Building an Information Security Awareness Program

Building an Information Security Awareness Program

Defending Against Social Engineering and Technical Threats

Bill Gardner

Valerie Thomas

AMSTERDAM • BOSTON • HEIDELBERG • LONDON
NEW YORK • OXFORD • PARIS • SAN DIEGO
SAN FRANCISCO • SINGAPORE • SYDNEY • TOKYO

Syngress is an Imprint of Elsevier

ELSEVIER

Acquiring Editor: *Chris Katsaropoulos*
Editorial Project Manager: *Benjamin Rearick*
Project Manager: *Punithavathy Govindaradjane*
Designer: *Mark Rogers*

Syngress is an imprint of Elsevier
225 Wyman Street, Waltham, MA 02451, USA

Library of Congress Cataloging-in-Publication Data
Gardner, Bill (Bill G.)
  Building an information security awareness program : defending against social engineering and technical threats / Bill Gardner, Valerie Thomas.
      pages cm
  Includes bibliographical references and index.
  ISBN 978-0-12-419967-5 (paperback)
1. Information storage and retrieval systems–Security measures. 2. Online social networks–Security measures. 3. Safety education. 4. Occupational training. 5. Situational awareness. I. Thomas, Valerie (Information security consultant) II. Title.
  TK5102.85.G37 2014
  658.3'1244–dc23

2014025010

British Library Cataloguing-in-Publication Data
A catalogue record for this book is available from the British Library

ISBN: 978-0-12-419967-5

For information on all Syngress publications,
visit our website at *store.elsevier.com/Syngress*

This book has been manufactured using Print On Demand technology. Each copy is produced to order and is limited to black ink. The online version of this book will show color figures where appropriate.

Working together
to grow libraries in
developing countries

www.elsevier.com • www.bookaid.org

Dedications

This book is dedicated to the love of my life and my best friend Blair Gardner and to my sister Kim Gardner.

–Bill Gardner

This book is dedicated to my family Chad, Andrew, and Lily and my grandmother Laura who inspired my love of reading.

–Valerie Thomas

Contents

Forewords

Companies invest millions of dollars each year in the latest security products, from firewalls to access-card systems, but they fail to invest in their most valuable resources in securing their environments—more specifically, their employees. All too often, security-awareness training is a once-a-year event involving dated and unengaging material that is largely ignored. The result is that employees lack understanding of modern-day attacks and their ramifications. This knowledge gap presents endless opportunities for attackers. In *Building a Security Awareness Program,* Bill Gardner and Valerie Thomas have detailed the steps for building an entire security-awareness program from scratch. The book also serves as a guidebook for those seeking to improve or modernize their existing security-awareness programs.

Personally, I have used this knowledge gap to my advantage in my past life as a black-hat hacker and throughout my time as a security consultant. I have accessed thousands of systems by combining social engineering with technical attacks. During a recent penetration test, I obtained access to a client's network by e-mailing a malicious document that appeared to originate from one of the client's vendors. All it took was one click of a mouse and I was in. A few days later, I had access to the client's entire corporate network, source code, financials, and more.

While phishing is a popular attack vector, other types of attacks still pose threats. The stories in the social engineering chapter may seem too good to be true, but they describe actual events. Thomas and Gardner have performed these attacks during penetration tests on unsuspecting employees and were successful every time. The best technologies in the world won't protect you if an attacker can walk right through the front door unchallenged. In Chapter 12, "Bringing It All Together," Thomas and Gardner define the steps needed not only to build an awareness program but also to begin the process of empowering the employee to challenge and verify suspicious behavior.

As attacks become more focused, organizations must adapt their defenses to include the human element of security. Creating an awareness program from the ground up can be intimidating and overwhelming. *Building a Security*

Awareness Program walks you through the step-by-step process of creating a program as unique as your organization so you'll be prepared when an attacker comes calling.

—Kevin Mitnick
speaker, consultant, and author of
The *New York Times* best-seller *Ghost in the Wires*

This book to me is one of the fundamental books that should be used in building an information security program and understanding what risks are really out there. For me, one of the largest risks we face in security today is through the human element. Bill and Valerie have done an amazing job in showing both the effectiveness of the types of attacks that can happen and most importantly how to build a successful program that aims at reducing the risks associated with targeted attacks. When I was a chief security officer for a Fortune 1000, building an education and awareness program was one of my most accomplishing moments. Not only did the awareness program give the security team an elevated detection capability with our employee population, but also it started to change the culture to something that was security-driven. When we implemented something in our organization, it wasn't because security was doing it to be draconian or overprotective—our employees actually understood that it was part of a much larger picture. A mission that mattered. Our program skyrocketed and moved at an escalated pace with executives and IT working for one goal alike. All because of our awareness program.

Flash forward and look at the attacks that are occurring. Our perimeter is getting better and we're locking down more things. Hackers move to the past of least resistance and that is our end-user population right now. We have to take action, we have to train our people, and most importantly, it has to matter to them. Education and awareness works, and I can prove it with folks that we work with all the time. I've seen awareness transform an entire company to be a security-driven one on a number of occasions. Focus less on the technology, and focus on the fundamental blocks of educating your users.

I've read a lot of books in my time, but this one is different. It's a way to build a successful security-awareness program, a way to pave your INFOSEC program forward, and a way to train users in a way that makes it possible to detect attacks. I'm such a big advocate on bringing awareness to corporations and employees; it's one of the most returns you will ever get on an investment. The blend that Bill and Valerie bring on showing successful attacks that have occurred in the wild and following it up with how to proactively defend is brilliant.

If you have read through this book already, take everything in, take a break, and figure out how to implement everything that you've learned here. These words of advice come from experience and what works. Your program, your visibility, and your ability to stop attacks while reducing risk depends on it.

If you are just picking this book up and you can pick up one book this year, pick this one. It's one of the most important books you will ever read.

—**Dave Kennedy**
speaker, consultant, author,
and CEO of TrustedSec

Preface

Many people have asked me why I wanted to write a book on building an information security awareness program. While everyone knows having one is a great idea, no one really knows where to start. The purpose of this book is to lay out a plan to build a program from the ground up and then look at some way to measure the effectiveness of the program once it's in place.

This book is meant to be a roadmap. One size won't always fit all, and there may be different routes to achieving the same goals in your organization. As I built information security awareness programs, I realized that documenting what I was doing and how I was doing it might be valuable to others who might need such information.

–**Bill Gardner**

About the Authors

Bill Gardner, OSCP, Sec+, and iNet+, is an assistant professor of Digital Forensics and Information Assurance at Marshall University, cofounder of 304Geeks and Hack3rcon, past president and board member at the Appalachian Institute of Digital Evidence (AIDE), and a member of the Security Awareness Training Framework.

Valerie Thomas is a senior information security consultant for Securicon LLC that specializes in social engineering and physical penetration testing. After obtaining her bachelor's degree in electronic engineering, Valerie led information security assessments for the Defense Information Systems Agency (DISA) before joining private industry. Throughout her career, Valerie has conducted penetration tests, vulnerability assessments, compliance audits, and technical security training for executives, developers, and other security professionals.

Acknowledgments

Thanks to the team at Syngress for making this book possible. I also want to thank the members of the Security Awareness Framework team for allowing me to bounce ideas off of them and taking part in the Q&A contained in the book. Thanks to Justin Brown and Frank Hackett for their support and help in developing ideas. Thanks to the 304Geeks, Rob Dixon, Matt Perry, Benny Karnes, and Rick Hayes for their support. Also, thanks to the guys in my "hacking crew": pr1me, gl1tch, c0ncelled, spridel, and Hackett. Thanks to the guys and gals at Hackers for Charity: Sam, Glenn, Nathan, Mary, and especially Johnny Long for their friendship and support. Also, thanks to Dave Kennedy for his friendship and being an example of someone who is a true leader and an inspiration. Thanks to Amanda Berlin, Phil Grimes, Jimmy Vo, Tess Schrodinger, and other contributors who took the time to contribute their knowledge and experience in the form of a Q&A that is included in this book.

Thanks to the many conference organizers who have let me talk about this subject at their conferences: Grecs at ShmooCon FireTalks; Adrian Crenshaw, Martin Bos, Dave Kennedy, Erin Kennedy, and Nich Hitchcock at DerbyCon; John Sammons, Jill Macintyre, Terry Fenger, Peggy Brown, and Kelly Griffith at AIDE; Liam Randall, Justin Hall, and the rest of the organizers at BsidesCincy; the organizers of BsidesCleveland; and the organizers of BsidesAsheville. Thanks to my online gang: George V. Hulme, Bill Brenner, Boris Sverdlik, Brian Martin of Digital Trust, KC Yerid, Leonard Isham, and Gal Shpantzer for keeping me entertained while I researched and wrote this book. Thanks to Lee Baird for his encouragement and support.

Thanks to John Sammons who put me in touch with the good folk at Syngress. Thanks to Branden Miller who I copresented my first talk on this subject at BsidesCleveland and DerbyCon. Thanks to my coauthor Valerie Thomas for coming aboard after the book had already started. Thanks to Krista McCallister for her help in double-checking my editing and research.

Thanks to my students who make me feel young and old at the same time; my colleagues, coworkers, and administration at Marshall University; the

West Virginia State University Economic Development Center who let me use their coworking space; Moxxee Coffee for letting me use their coffee shop as a writing space; my friend Kara Stevens for going to lunch with me providing breaks from long writing days; and Infected Mushroom and Dual Core who provided the soundtrack for writing the book. A big thanks to Dave Kennedy and Kevin Mitnick for writing the forwards for this book.

Thanks to my family, my mother Betty, my niece Amber, my late sister Kim, my late father Bill, my grandfather Bill Hammonds, and the rest of my family.

An extra thanks to Blair Gardner who put up my long days and nights spent at my computer. Without your love and support, this book would not have been possible.

–**Bill Gardner**

Apart from the efforts of myself, the success of this book depends largely on the encouragement and support of many others. Thank you to my husband Chad and children Andrew and Lily for their patience and support during the many hours glued to my keyboard. I promise to take a break now. A special thanks to my parents who saved the little storybooks that I wrote at the age of 7; hopefully, this is more impressive. I would like to thank Syngress and my coauthor Bill Gardner for making this publication possible. Thanks to Tim Lawton, Jay Llewellyn, and Danielle Dominguez for helping me in the content review and editing process. Thank you to my friend, Kevin Mitnick, for writing the foreword for this book. It's been many years since I first opened *The Art of Deception*, which inspired my career in information security, and I can't thank you enough for your inspiration and support. I would also like to thank Dave Kennedy for also contributing a foreword to this book and for being an inspiration to all of us in the security industry. Thanks to my friend and mentor Chris Russo, who always helped me find my way.

–**Valerie Thomas**

CHAPTER 1

What Is a Security Awareness Program?

Bill Gardner
Marshall University, Huntington, WV, USA

INTRODUCTION

A security awareness program is a formal program with the goal of training users of the potential threats to an organization's information and how to avoid situations that might put the organization's data at risk.

The goals of the security awareness program are to lower the organization's attack surface, to empower users to take personal responsibility for protecting the organization's information, and to enforce the policies and procedures the organization has in place to protect its data. Policies and procedures might include but are not limited to computer use policies, Internet use policies, remote access policies, and other policies that aim to govern and protect the organization's data.

In information security, people are the weakest link. People want to be helpful. People want to do a good job. People want to give good customer service to their coworkers, clients, and vendors. People are curious. Social engineers seek to exploit these characteristics in humans. "Social Engineering is defined as the process of deceiving people into giving away access or confidential information" [1]. The only known defense for social engineering attacks is an effective security awareness program. Unless users understand the tactics and techniques of social engineers, they will fall prey and put the organization's data at risk.

A survey of recent breaches will reveal that a large majority of them took advantage of exploiting humans. One example is the RSA breach [2] where sophisticated attackers used targeted spear phishing to steal RSA SecurID authentication tokens that lead to a further breach at US defense contractor Lockheed Martin [3]. Another example is the "Aurora" attack against Google and other large software companies that used an attack that sent users to a website that infected users with a cutting-edge 0day exploit. The result was that a large amount of intellectual property including source code was stolen from companies including Google and Adobe [4].

Nowadays, online bad guys don't try to break in through the firewall. Bad guys go around the firewall. Organizations have spent billions of dollars developing layered defenses against online attackers. There are solutions such as antivirus, intrusion detection systems, intrusion prevention systems, and other technical solutions to protect information. With these sophisticated solutions in place, attackers are now turning to more targeted attacks focused on tricking users into clicking links or opening attachments.

Dave Kennedy's Social-Engineer Toolkit does an excellent job of modeling social engineer attacks such as website, attachment, human interface device (HID), and QR attacks for defenders to use to test their own environments [5]. This might sound simplistic, but what would most users do if they received an attachment that appears to come from the HR department that appears to be a spreadsheet of raises for everyone in the organization (Figure 1.1)? Curiosity might not just kill the cat; it might also put your data at risk.

While SET is a technical tool, its goal is to use nontechnical means to exploit humans who in turn exploit computers, which leads to data compromise [6]. SET can easily clone a website to an attacker's machine where exploits are then inserted into the website. At that point, the attacker will attempt to direct users to the cloned site. This might be accomplished by spear phishing, sending the user linked disguised by a link-shortening service or buying a domain to host the cloned site that looks legitimate. Once the user is on the cloned site, the attacker can use a number of different attack vectors to steal information or install backdoors to allow the attack to access the system as if the attacker was a legitimate user. SET also has the ability to encode these attacks, so they are not detected by antivirus and other software used to detect malware and intrusions. The credential harvester attack is accomplished through SET by cloning a site like Twitter, Facebook, or even a bank or credit card site with a username and password file. When the user attempts to log into the site, SET steals the username and password and logs the user into the legitimate website. We will discuss SET in more detail later in the book.

A security awareness program also is a building block of a mature security program. Policies and procedures are the first building blocks. The next layer is a security awareness program, also called user awareness training. Only when these two elements are in place do we then move to the next steps of patch management, log management, antivirus/HIDS, security appliances, and finally metrics. For years, organizations have thrown money at security, when that money would have been better spent training their users (Figure 1.2). The focus of this book is building a security awareness program step by step with the ultimate goal of building a mature security program.

FIGURE 1.1 Social-Engineer Toolkit (SET).

FIGURE 1.2 Elements of a mature security program.

POLICY DEVELOPMENT

Policy development sets the goals, limitations, and expectations of the organization's users. Depending on the size of the organization, these policies can be a number of documents addressing specific divisions of the organization's IT and HR structure, or it might in the case of smaller organizations be one single document that outlines the limitations and duties of those who use the organization's telephone, computer, e-mail, and other digital assets.

The most common policy is the computer use policy. Other separate policies that can be addressed in a separate document are e-mail usage, Internet usage, telephone usage, and fax usage. Computer use, also sometimes called acceptable use policy, defines the user's level of access to computer and telecommunication resources and their rights and limitation as to the use of those resources. The biggest goal of the acceptable use is to define where use ends and abuse begins. For example, it would be deemed an abuse in most organizations if user spends work time accessing porn and gambling sites. It would also be considered abuse if employees use phone and e-mail services for excessive personal communication during the workday. Most organizations understand that some personal use is necessary and the acceptable use policy to define what constitutes what is acceptable and what is not acceptable use of the organization's equipment and services.

Some organizations' usage policies are based on the template found on the Internet [7]. While these sorts of templates are useful, it is important to remember that they need to be customized to define the needs and missions of your organization.

The organization's human resources department also needs to be involved. In many cases, specific portions of the policies will have penalties that will be enforced by HR. In most cases, policies and procedure will have to be developed with regulations in mind. Those organizations that handle health data are likely to be covered by HIPAA/HITECH. Organizations that handle credit card transactions are likely to be covered by PCI DSS. Specifically, the HIPAA/HITECH physical standards of the security rule address issues including workstation use, 164.310(b); workstation security, 164.310(c); and device and media controls, 164.310(d)(1). HIPAA/HITECH also calls for punishing those who don't follow policies under the administrative standards of the security rule, specifically authorizations and/or supervision, workforce clearance procedure, and termination procedures, 164.308(a)(3).

POLICY ENFORCEMENT

Policy without enforcement is a waste of time and a detriment to the organization. One of the goals of an effective security awareness program is to enforce policies by educating users on what the policies and the organization's expectations are.

There is nothing more useless than an unenforced policy. Many organizations spend a lot of time developing policies. Many times, these policies end up in a binder on a shelf in someone's office.

Giving copies of the acceptable use and other policies to the users is a good first step, but most of the time, the users will not spend the time to read the information. A security awareness program should be used to review these policies, especially the policies that apply to the use, abuse, and penalties for the abuse of the organization's communication and information technology infrastructure.

The goal of this book is to illustrate how to build an effective security awareness program from getting management buy-in to measuring the program using effective metrics. It is also written for anyone from a managerial level to the IT manager on the digital frontlines with an interest in starting a security awareness program. While we will be covering a lot of ground in this book, the end goal is for you to be able to develop an engaging security awareness program that will help your organization manage its risk when it comes to online threats.

COST SAVINGS

Data breaches cost money. If you are an organization covered by regulations such as HIPAA/HITECH or PCI DSS, the penalties for data breaches could be millions of dollars depending on the size of the breach. Additionally, many states now have breach notification laws that require organizations that lose data to inform those affected as to what was lost and in some cases provide credit protection to those affected. Ponemon Institute and Symantec released a report in June of 2013 that found that breaches in 2012 cost an average of $136 per record globally [8].

In May 2012, the US Department of Health and Human Services Office of Civil Rights fined the Idaho State University $400 K for health data breaches [9]. In June 2012, the Alaska Department of Health and Human Services (DHHS) agreed to pay $1.7 million to settle potential violations of HIPAA/HITECH [10].

The payment card industry has established fines of up to $500,000 per incident for data breaches [11]. In 2010, Genesco, a Nashville, TN-based sportswear company, was fined more than $13 million dollars for noncompliance with PCI DSS regulations after the firm discovered they had been hacked and regulators discovered noncompliance [12].

PRODUCTION INCREASES

Less malware and computer problems can lead to less downtime and increased production in organizations. IT and security teams can actually spend time being proactive and moving the organization's mission forward instead of reactively responding to viruses and other malware infections and investigating possible actual data breaches [13].

Some infections and breaches can lead to days or possibly weeks of downtime. These sorts of disruptions lead to decreased profits for the organization and in some cases expose the organization to civil legal action, possible regulatory action, and possible loss of clients and business partners.

Some data breaches are not the result of an outside actor but are rather the mistake of an employee such as turning off a firewall [14] or not properly configuring a website to not display confidential data to the public [15]. Without the knowledge to properly do their jobs, employees continue to make mistakes.

The ultimate goal of a security awareness program is to manage an organization's risk. Most organizations have safety programs to keep employees safe at work. The goal of a security awareness program should be to keep an organization's data safe.

MANAGEMENT BUY-IN

The first and most important step to building a security awareness program is getting the approval and support of the management structure of the organizations. Without managerial support, policies will go unwritten, policies will go unenforced, and management and employees will rebel against any structure, rules, or limitations being put on them in regard to securing the organization's information. Even in the face of regulations such as HIPAA/HITECH and PCI DSS, without support from the management of the organizations, security awareness indicatives will fail.

Management buy-in begins by demonstrating risk to management and then illustrating how a security awareness program will help them manage that risk. The second step is to show management how such a program can support the business goals of the organization including policy development, policy enforcement, cost savings, and production increases.

Illustrating risk includes case studies that are specific to the organization's industry. For example, if your organization is a law firm, use case studies and examples of lawyers and law firms that have been breached because of mistakes made by users. It is also important to illustrate the cunningness of attackers. Most people think of everyday nontargeted virus infections when they think of security, when the most dangerous attackers are technically advanced hackers looking to steal intellectual property, financial information, and trade secrets.

Management is not always receptive to change, especially when they think that such changes will get in the way of the business goals of the organization. Properly communicating with management in nontechnical terms is key to getting management buy-in. When managers from the top down understand the purposes and goals of a security awareness program and that such a program is in line with the business goals of the organization, mainly making money, they will be more receptive to implementing a security awareness program.

For the remainder of this book, we will continue to look at the specific step to a security awareness program from scratch with little or no money. Common sense approaches are the best way to combat a large number of modern threats to information. While some organizations offer paid, often canned security awareness programs, the focus of this book is to empower the reason to build their own program within their own organizations whether those organizations are small, medium, or large businesses or corporations or if they are nonprofit groups or even schools. Most of this information will also be useable by home users to better manage their risk when facing online threats, but home users are beyond the scope of this book.

Notes

[1] Social Engineering Framework. http://www.social-engineer.org/framework/Social_Engineering_Defined [accessed on 02.06.13].

[2] Digital Dao: Evolving Hostilities in the Global Cyber Commons. http://jeffreycarr.blogspot.com/2011/06/18-days-from-0day-to-8k-rsa-attack.html [accessed on 03.06.13].

[3] InformationWeek Security: RSA Breach: Eight Months Later. http://www.informationweek.com/security/attacks/rsa-breach-eight-months-later/231903048 [accessed on 03.06.13].

[4] Wired: Google Hack Attack Was Ultra Sophisticated, New Details Show. http://www.wired.com/threatlevel/2010/01/operation-aurora/ [accessed on 03.06.13].

[5] TrustedSec: Social Engineer Toolkit. https://www.trustedsec.com/downloads/social-engineer-toolkit/ [accessed on 04.06.13].

[6] Social Engineering Framework: Computer Based Social Engineering Tools: Social Engineer Toolkit (SET). http://www.social-engineer.org/framework/Computer_Based_Social_Engineering_Tools:_Social_Engineer_Toolkit_(SET) [accessed on 04.06.13]

[7] SANS: Information Security Policy Templates. http://www.sans.org/security-resources/policies/ [accessed on 04.06.13].

[8] Ponemon and Symantec Find Most Data Breaches Caused by Human and System Errors. http://www.symantec.com/about/news/release/article.jsp?prid=20130605_01&om_ext_cid=biz_socmed_twitter_facebook_marketwire_linkedin_2013Jun_worldwide_CostofaDataBreach [accessed on 05.06.13].

[9] HHS fines Idaho State University $400 K for health data breach. http://healthitsecurity.com/2013/05/22/hhs-fines-idaho-state-university-400k-for-data-breach/ [accessed on 06.06.13].

[10] Alaska DHSS settles HIPAA security case for $1,700,000. http://www.hhs.gov/ocr/privacy/hipaa/enforcement/examples/alaska-agreement.html [accessed on 06.06.13].

[11] PCI-DSS: Security—Penalties. https://financial.ucsc.edu/Pages/Security_Penalties.aspx [accessed on 06.06.13].

[12] Retailer fights PCI fines for noncompliance after breach, sues Visa. http://www.scmagazine.com/retailer-fights-pci-fines-for-noncompliance-after-breach-sues-visa/article/284088/ [accessed on 06.06.13].

[13] Downtime Rated Top Risk Of Data Breaches. http://www.informationweek.com/security/management/downtime-rated-top-risk-of-data-breaches/228201056 [accessed on 07.06.13].

[14] HHS fines Idaho State University $400 K for health data breach. http://healthitsecurity.com/2013/05/22/hhs-fines-idaho-state-university-400k-for-data-breach/ [accessed on 07.06.13].

[15] Brookhaven data breach 'was clerical error', officials say. http://www.newsday.com/long-island/towns/brookhaven-data-breach-was-clerical-error-officials-say-1.5426405 [accessed on 07.06.13].

CHAPTER 2

Threat

Bill Gardner
Marshall University, Huntington, WV, USA

THE MOTIVATIONS OF ONLINE ATTACKERS

In order to properly train user, the first order of business is to get them to understand the threats they face online, the threat actors, and the motivation of online criminals. Many times, users do not understand the value of the information they access every day to do their work. In the case of a law firm, the firm will have gathered a larger amount of confidential data to use representing the interests of their clients. In the case accounting firms, the firm has access to sensitive financial documents of their clients. Doctors, hospitals, and insurance companies have access to sensitive health data. Employers collect personal and financial information, such as social security numbers, and other personal information from their employees in order to process insurance and payroll. In the case of an employee with a family, the employer needs to collect the social security numbers and other personal information of family members.

Think about the information in your own organization. How much do you have to lose if your employer lost your personal and financial information? How much does your organization have to lose if it lost the confidential and privileged information it has been entrusted with by its employees, clients, and business partners?

MONEY

The chief goal of online attackers is money. Online criminals make billions of dollars from online schemes, fraud, and thievery [1]. Some groups target computers to steal personal information and credit card information [2]. Stolen credit card information can be either used directly or sold to other criminals.

9

INDUSTRIAL ESPIONAGE/TRADE SECRETS

Other more sophisticated attackers seek to steal confidential information and intellectual property for sale. If an online criminal could steal the formula for Coke, for example, they could sell it for a lot of money [3].

HACKTIVISM

Hacktivists are motivated by political causes [4]. The most widely known hacktivist group is Anonymous and its affiliated groups [5]. Hacktivism is defined as "the nonviolent use of illegal or legally ambiguous digital tools in pursuit of political ends. These tools include web site defacements, redirects, denial-of-service attacks, information theft..." [6].

There are many different examples of hacktivism, but the largest, most successful, and most well known was Operation Sony. Also known as Op Sony, the operation Anonymous calls their cause de jour was the case of George Hotz who is also known as the first hacker to "jailbreak" the iPhone. George, known online by his handle GeoHot, also wanted to "jailbreak" his PlayStation 3, which would allow users the ability to play and share homemade games. On December 29th, 2010, George Hotz and the rest of hacker collective known as fail0verflow announced they had retrieved the root key of Sony's PlayStation 3 gaming console at the 29th Chaos Communications Congress. On January 3rd, 2011, George Hotz published his findings on his website, geohot.com. On January 11th, 2011, Sony filed a lawsuit against George Hotz and other members of fail0verflow for releasing the PlayStation 3's root key [7].

In April 2011, Anonymous fired the first salvo in what came to be known as Op Sony, by taking the PlayStation Network (PSN) and several PlayStation-related domains, including the PlayStation Store, offline [8]. It was later learned that the attacks not only resulted in an outage of the PSN service but also turned out to be one of the largest data breaches in history involving over 70 million records including personally identifiable information (PII) and credit card information [9].

This period of time also saw the rise of a subgroup of Anonymous known as LulzSec. This brash subgroup of Anonymous ultimately took credit for stealing 24.6 million records in the PlayStation Network [10]. The group then went on an extensive hacking spree that involved a number of high-profile targets from Fox.com to PBS and the game company Bethesda Game Studios while tweaking the noses and taunting law enforcement the entire time. The group saw themselves as modern-day Robin Hoods that were exposing the insecurities of the websites they breached. As their hacking spree continued, they continued to garner public attention and the attention of law enforcement though the summer of 2011. The group's activities became more brazen and outlandish

[10]. By the beginning of the fall of 2011, the group began to unravel when it was reported that the group's leader Sabu, whose real name is Hector Xavier Monsegur, was arrested on June 7, 2011, and had turned FBI informant [11]. By the end of 2011, all the members of the LulzSec crew would be arrested and jailed. While the reign of the LulzSec crew had ended, the various groups known as Anonymous live on.

Anonymous got its start in 2003 on the Internet image site 4chan.org where each user posted as an Anonymous user. As the site evolved, many of the "Anonymous" users found that they had certain goals and political views in common. The message board on 4chan.org, mainly a message board called /b/, is for the posting of random information that contains calls to action. While Anonymous has been involved in a number of data breaches, they are mainly known for distributed denial-of-service (DDoS) attacks on government, religious, and corporate websites. Some of the high-profile targets of such attacks include the Westboro Baptist Church, Church of Scientology, PayPal, MasterCard, and Visa [12]. Many members of Anonymous learned of the Sony lawsuit against George Hotz on the site, and ongoing operations were often discussed and coordinated on 4chan, but Anonymous now shares operational details on Pastebin.com. Pastebin was developed as a site to share information for a certain period of time [13], but it's unclear that the developers ever dreamed that it would become the focal point of an ongoing Anonymous operation at it is today. Anonymous and Anonymous-associated hacking groups also use the site to dump personal information about their enemies, known in the Internet underworld as doxing, and share confidential information taken from data breaches such as e-mail, passwords, usernames, and password hashes.

CYBER WAR

Cyber war is defined as nation-state versus nation-state. In some cases, it appears that nation-states have used patriotic hackers and hacker gangs to further their national interest. We refer to these actions as cyber war as well. Cyber war has recently become a hot button issue, with most of the blame for intrusions being directed to the Chinese government. What we today call cyber war is not new. Titan Rain is the code name given to a series of coordinated attacks on American computer systems, attributed to the Chinese government, since 2003 by the US government [14].

One of the most talked about and widely cited incidents of cyber war happened in Estonia in 2007, when a disagreement with Russia over the relocation of the "Bronze Soldier of Tallinn" and war graves in Tallinn (the capital of Estonia) resulted in a series of massive coordinated cyber attacks on the Estonian public and private sectors. Estonian banks, parliament, ministries, newspapers, and TV were knocked offline [15].

Recently, the headlines have been filled with news about new types of targeted weapons being used in what we now call cyber war. The most notable of these new "cyber weapons" is Stuxnet [16]. Stuxnet targeted centrifuges at the Natanz uranium enrichment plant in Iran. The cyber attack set back the Iranian nuclear program years according to some experts. It also might have saved lives since conventional military action was not necessary to destroy the centrifuges [17].

A subset of cyber war is cyber espionage. It is the most immediate threat to businesses and other organizations. In September 2010, a number of Canadian-based law firms where reportedly breached by China-based hackers looking to derail the $40 billion acquisition of the world's largest potash producer by an Australian mining company [18]. On February 18, 2013, the Internet security firm Mandiant released a report, which claims that it has hard evidence that the Chinese army is behind supplicated intrusions into US networks to steal sensitive data and trade secrets from both governmental and nongovernmental organizations [19].

BRAGGING RIGHTS

Doing something other people say is impossible gives a hacker a lot of "cred" and followers in the digital underground. Reputation is currency in the dark world of Internet criminals. In 2011, hackers founded a site called "RankMyHack.com" (now offline) to score hacks. The more sophisticated the hack, the higher the score [20].

Long before hackers were stealing money and intellectual property, they were showing off to other hackers. While the common use of the word hacker today refers to someone who breaks into computers, the word originally came out the student culture at MIT in the 1970s. If a student came up with a particularly eloquent solution to a complicated problem in the fewest steps, they were called a hacker, and the solution was called a hack. Later, the word hacker was applied to complicated practical jokes the students played on the MIT administration. These pranks date back to 1947 when the students of MIT used primer cord to burn the letters MIT in the football field at Harvard. Other pranks included putting a replica of an MIT police car on top of a campus building complete with flashing blue lights [21].

Notes

[1] Sizing the Market for Cybercrime. http://www.guardiannetworksolutions.com/cyber-crime-costs/ [accessed on 13.06.13].

[2] The terrifying rise of cyber crime: Your computer is currently being targeted by criminal gangs looking to harvest your personal details and steal your money. http://www.dailymail.co.uk/home/moslive/article-2260221/Cyber-crime-Your-currently-targeted-criminal-gangs-looking-steal-money.html [accessed on 13.06.13].

[3] Has this man found the original recipe for Coca-Cola in an old drawer? Antiques dealer puts 'secret formula' on eBay for $15 MILLION. http://www.dailymail.co.uk/news/article-2324106/Coca-Cola-formula-Georgia-man-says-secret-1943-recipe-Coke.html [accessed on 13.06.13].

[4] Hacktivism: A Short History. http://www.foreignpolicy.com/articles/2013/04/29/hacktivism [accessed on 13.06.13].

[5] Anonymous: From the Lulz to Collective Action. http://mediacommons.futureofthebook.org/tne/pieces/anonymous-lulz-collective-action [accessed on 21.05.14].

[6] Hacktivism and the Future of Political Participation. http://www.alexandrasamuel.com/dissertation/index.html [accessed on 18.06.13].

[7] Know Your Meme: Operation Sony. http://knowyourmeme.com/memes/events/operation-sony [accessed on 18.06.13].

[8] Anonymous' Operation: Sony is a double-edged sword. http://www.thetechherald.com/articles/Anonymous-Operation-Sony-is-a-double-edged-sword/13239/ [accessed on 18.06.13].

[9] Security experts: PlayStation Network breach one of largest ever. http://content.usatoday.com/communities/gamehunters/post/2011/04/security-experts-playstation-network-breach-one-of-largest-ever/1#.UcD1ufZgahg [accessed on 18.06.13].

[10] LulzSec: what they did, who they were and how they were caught. http://www.guardian.co.uk/technology/2013/may/16/lulzsec-hacking-fbi-jail [accessed on 18.06.13].

[11] LulzSec Leader Betrays All of Anonymous. http://gizmodo.com/5890825/lulzsec-leader-betrays-all-of-anonymous [accessed on 21.05.14].

[12] SERIOUS BUSINESS: Anonymous Takes On Scientology (and Doesn't Afraid of Anything) http://www2.citypaper.com/columns/story.asp?id=15543 [accessed on 21.05.14].

[13] Pastebin Surpasses 10 Million "Active" Pastes. http://techcrunch.com/2011/10/26/pastebin-surpasses-10-million-active-pastes/?utm_source=feedburner&utm_medium=feed&utm_campaign=Feed%3A+Techcrunch+%28TechCrunch%29 [accessed on 21.05.14].

[14] Security experts lift lid on Chinese hack attacks. http://web.archive.org/web/20061211145201/http://news.zdnet.com/2100-1009_22-5969516.html [accessed on 21.05.14].

[15] Estonia's Lessons in Cyberwarfare. http://www.usnews.com/opinion/blogs/world-report/2013/01/14/estonia-shows-how-to-build-a-defense-against-cyberwarfare [accessed on 23.06.13].

[16] Legal Experts: Stuxnet Attack on Iran Was Illegal 'Act of Force'. http://www.wired.com/threatlevel/2013/03/stuxnet-act-of-force/ [accessed on 22.06.13].

[17] Did a U.S. Government Lab Help Israel Develop Stuxnet?. http://www.wired.com/threatlevel/2011/01/inl-and-stuxnet/all/ [accessed on 22.06.13].

[18] China-Based Hackers Target Law Firms to Get Secret Deal Data. http://www.bloomberg.com/news/2012-01-31/china-based-hackers-target-law-firms.html [accessed on 22.06.13].

[19] APT1 Three Months Later - Significantly Impacted, Though Active & Rebuilding. https://www.mandiant.com/blog/apt1-months-significantly-impacted-active-rebuilding/ [accessed on 22.06.13].

[20] Web Site Ranks Hacks and Bestows Bragging Rights http://www.nytimes.com/2011/08/22/technology/web-site-ranks-hacks-and-bestows-bragging-rights.html [accessed on 23.06.13].

[21] Hacks on the Great Dome (Bldg. 10). http://hacks.mit.edu/Hacks/by_location/great_dome.html [accessed on 21.05.14].

CHAPTER 3

Cost of a Data Breach

Bill Gardner

Marshall University, Huntington, WV, USA

PONEMON INSTITUTE

There are a number of institutions that track information related to the cost of data breaches, but the only organization that devotes its entire time and budget to tracking data breach costs is the Ponemon Institute (http://www.ponemon. org/). According to the current research, the per record cost of data breaches averaged $194.00 in the United States. The Ponemon Institute in partnership with Symantec released "Ponemon Cost of Data Breach 2013" in May 2013 [1]. The report covers data collected worldwide and is further broken down by country.

HIPAA

In the United States, the costs of breaches are from paying regulatory fines, mandatory notification of affected parties, and lost of business due to customer lost of trust. Figures for fines for violating HIPAA alone have resulted in millions of dollars [2] of fines for covered entities.

A covered entity is defined as an organization that has a role in handling medical records including doctors, clinics, dentists, psychologists, chiropractors, and nursing homes. Also included in the definition are health plans such as medical, dental, and vision plans and health-care clearinghouses that handle health data such as billing and collection companies [3].

Covered entities are subject to the HIPAA Security Rule. The HIPAA Security Rule applies to any protected health information (PHI) that is in an electronic state. Not all specifications from the Security Rule are required. Some are "addressable," meaning that a covered entity can further assess whether the specification is reasonable and appropriate for the organization. The term

15

addressable does not mean that the specification is optional; rather, it means if it's reasonable based on the size and make-up of the organization. Whether required or addressable, you should carefully document implementation choices [4].

The compliance deadline for the HIPAA Security Rule, finalized and published on February 20, was February 21, 2005. If you were required to comply with the Privacy Rule or Electronic Transactions and Code Sets Rule, you are a "covered entity" and must also comply with the Security Rule.

The Department of Health and Human Services (DHHS) provides flexibility to covered entities by stating whether a specification is "required" or "addressable."

If the specification is "required," the covered entity must implement the specification as stated in the Security Rule.

If the specification is "addressable," then the covered entity must do the following:

1. Assess whether the specification is a reasonable and appropriate safeguard in its environment and is likely to contribute to protecting the entity's electronically protected health information.
2. Implement the specification or document why it would not be reasonable and appropriate and implement an equivalent alternative measure if reasonable and appropriate.

Implementation specifications

(R) = required, (A) = addressable

Administrative safeguards

Standards

Security management process

- Risk analysis (R)
- Risk management (R)
- Sanction policy (R)
- Information system activity review (R)

Assigned security responsibility (R)

Workforce security

- Authorization and/or supervision (A)
- Workforce clearance procedure (A)
- Termination procedures (A)

Information access management

- Isolating health-care clearinghouse function (R)
- Access authorization (A)
- Access establishment and modification (A)

Security awareness and training

- Security reminders (A)
- Protection from malicious software (A)
- Log-in monitoring (A)
- Password management (A)

Security incident procedures

- Response and reporting (R)

Contingency plan

- Data backup plan (R)
- Disaster recovery plan (R)
- Emergency mode operation plan (R)
- Testing and revision procedure (A)
- Applications and data criticality analysis (A)

Evaluation (R)

Business associate contracts and other arrangements

- Written contract or other arrangements (R)

Physical safeguards

Standards

Facility access controls

- Contingency operations (A)
- Facility security plan (A)
- Access control and validation procedures (A)
- Maintenance records (A)

Workstation use (R)

Workstation security (R)

Device and media controls

- Disposal (R)
- Media reuse (R)
- Accountability (A)
- Data backup and storage (A)

Technical safeguards

Standards

Access control

- Unique user identification (R)
- Emergency access procedure (R)
- Automatic logoff (A)
- Encryption and decryption (A)

Audit controls (R)

Integrity

- Mechanism to authenticate electronic PHI (A)

Person or entity authentication (R)

Transmission security

- Integrity controls (A)
- Encryption (A)

Organizational safeguards

Standards

Business associate contracts or other arrangements (R)

Group health plans (R)

Policies and procedures (R)

Documentation

- Time limit (R)
- Availability (R)
- Updates (R)

While "Security Awareness and Training" is "addressable" under the HIPAA Security Rule [5], it doesn't mean that your organization should go without it. In many cases, as you review regulations specific to your organization, you will find that regulations only go so far. Many only address the bare minimum of what it takes to make your organization secure. It has been repeated time and time again that complying with government and industry regulations alone will not make your organization secure, but it will save you a lot of money and is often an important first step to building a mature security program.

My former colleague Bob Coffield covered one recent large fine related to violation of the HIPAA Security Rule in his "Health Care Law Blog":

"The HHS Office for Civil Rights (OCR) announced a settlement of $1.5M with Blue Cross Blue Shield of Tennessee (BCBST) relating to potential violations under the HIPAA Privacy and Security Rules. According to the OCR press release, the enforcement action by OCR is the first reported as resulting from a breach report required under the new Breach Notification Rule implemented as a result of the HITECH provisions of HIPAA.

The breach involved 57 unencrypted computer hard drives that were stolen from a facility leased by BCBST in Tennessee. The hard drives contained protected health information of approximately 1 million individuals. The breach was reported by BCBST to OCR under the HITECH provisions and regulations that require reporting of potential breaches. The press release indicates that OCRs investigation found that BCBST failed to implement appropriate administrative safeguards to adequately protect information remaining at the leased facility by not performing the required security evaluation in response to operational changes. In addition, the investigation showed a failure to implement appropriate physical safeguards by not having adequate facility access controls; both of these safeguards are required by the HIPAA Security Rule" [6].

THE PAYMENT CARD INDUSTRY DATA SECURITY STANDARD (PCI DSS)

Another regulation covering data breaches is PCI DSS.

"The Payment Card Industry Data Security Standard (PCI DSS) is a proprietary information security standard for organizations that handle cardholder information for the major debit, credit, prepaid, e-purse, ATM, and POS cards."

"Defined by the Payment Card Industry Security Standards Council, the standard was created to increase controls around cardholder data to reduce credit card fraud via its exposure. Validation of compliance is done annually — by an external Qualified Security Assessor (QSA) that creates a Report on Compliance (ROC) for organizations handling large volumes of transactions, or by Self-Assessment Questionnaire (SAQ) for companies handling smaller volumes" [7].

PCI DSS to many was a reaction to the TJX data breach, which at the time was the largest and most expensive breach in history. According to accounts, 45 million customer credit and debit card numbers were taken by criminals in the breach. The total cost, including litigation costs and the cost to fix the issues that lead to the breach, to cardholders, banks, and the credit card industry is estimated to be $256 million [8].

According to the 2012 Verizon Data Breach Investigation Report, 96% of the merchants experiencing a data breach in 2011 had not complied with the PCI DSS [9]. According to the 2011 Cost of Data Breach Study, direct cost associated with recovering from a security breach average in 2011 was $194 per stolen record [10]. Since the typical breach involves tens of thousands of records, the results can be catastrophic to a business [11].

HIPAA and PCI DSS are just two examples of regulations that might affect your organization. Become familiar with the regulations in your field, and make sure you include them in your security awareness training.

STATE BREACH NOTIFICATION LAWS

A number of states of now enacted breach notification laws that result in data breach cost over and above regulations such as HIPAA, SOX, and PCI DSS. According to the National Conference of State Legislatures (NCSL), 46 states, the District of Columbia, Guam, Puerto Rico, and the Virgin Islands have enacted breach notification laws [12]. Breach notification laws were enacted as a result of a number of high-profile data breaches such as the much-covered TJX breach.

The ideas behind the laws were to give consumers notification and credit protection in the event customers' data have been lost. Not providing notification and credit protection can result in large fines to the organization that lost the data via thief or negligence. In the case of a loss, an organization's first duty is to determine what has been lost: social security, credit card information, home address, date of birth, or other personally identifiable information (PII). Each state has different triggers for the laws. Common criteria include a number of records and the type of data lost [13].

Below is the breach notification law for the state of West Virginia, which is typical of other state breach notification laws:

CHAPTER 46A. WEST VIRGINIA CONSUMER CREDIT AND PROTECTION ACT.

Article 2A. Breach of Security of Consumer Information.

§46A-2A-101. Definitions

As used in this article:

(1) "Breach of the security of a system" means the unauthorized access and acquisition of unencrypted and unredacted computerized data that compromises the security or

confidentiality of personal information maintained by an individual or entity as part of a database of personal information regarding multiple individuals and that causes the individual or entity to reasonably believe that the breach of security has caused or will cause identity theft or other fraud to any resident of this state. Good faith acquisition of personal information by an employee or agent of an individual or entity for the purposes of the individual or the entity is not a breach of the security of the system, provided that the personal information is not used for a purpose other than a lawful purpose of the individual or entity or subject to further unauthorized disclosure.

(2) "Entity" includes corporations, business trusts, estates, partnerships, limited partnerships, limited liability partnerships, limited liability companies, associations, organizations, joint ventures, governments, governmental subdivisions, agencies or instrumentalities, or any other legal entity, whether for profit or not for profit.

(3) "Encrypted" means transformation of data through the use of an algorithmic process to into a form in which there is a low probability of assigning meaning without use of a confidential process or key or securing the information by another method that renders the data elements unreadable or unusable.

(4) "Financial institution" has the meaning given that term in Section 6809(3), United States Code Title 15, as amended.

(5) "Individual" means a natural person.

(6) "Personal information" means the first name or first initial and last name linked to any one or more of the following data elements that relate to a resident of this state, when the data elements are neither encrypted nor redacted:

(A) Social security number;

(B) Driver's license number or state identification card number issued in lieu of a driver's license; or

(C) Financial account number, or credit card, or debit card number in combination with any required security code, access code, or password that would permit access to a resident's financial accounts.

The term does not include information that is lawfully obtained from publicly available information, or from federal, state or local government records lawfully made available to the general public.

(7) "Notice" means:

(A) Written notice to the postal address in the records of the individual or entity;

(B) Telephonic notice;

(C) Electronic notice, if the notice provided is consistent with the provisions regarding electronic records and signatures, set forth in Section 7001, United States Code Title 15, Electronic Signatures in Global and National Commerce Act.

(D) Substitute notice, if the individual or the entity required to provide notice demonstrates that the cost of providing notice will exceed fifty thousand dollars or that the affected class of residents to be notified exceeds one hundred thousand persons or that the individual or the entity does not have sufficient contact information or to provide notice as described in paragraph (A), (B), or (C). Substitute notice consists of any two of the following:

(i) E-mail notice if the individual or the entity has e-mail addresses for the members of the affected class of residents;

(ii) Conspicuous posting of the notice on the website of the individual or the entity if the individual or the entity maintains a website; or

(iii) Notice to major statewide media.

(8) "Redact" means alteration or truncation of data such that no more than the last four digits of a social security number, driver's license number, state identification card number, or account number is accessible as part of the personal information.

§46A-2A-102. Notice of breach of security of computerized personal information

(a) An individual or entity that owns or licenses computerized data that includes personal information shall give notice of any breach of the security of the system following discovery or notification of the breach of the security of the system to any resident of this state whose unencrypted and unredacted personal information was or is reasonably believed to have been accessed and acquired by an unauthorized person and that causes, or the individual, or entity reasonably believes has caused or will cause, identity theft, or other fraud to any resident of this state. Except as provided in subsection (e) of this section or in order to take any measures necessary to determine the scope of the breach and to restore the reasonable integrity of the system, the notice shall be made without unreasonable delay.

(b) An individual or entity must give notice of the breach of the security of the system if encrypted information is accessed and acquired in an unencrypted form or if the security breach involves a person with access to the encryption key and the individual or entity reasonably believes that such breach has caused or will cause identity theft or other fraud to any resident of this state.

(c) An individual or entity that maintains computerized data that includes personal information that the individual or entity does not own or license shall give notice to the owner or licensee of the information of any breach of the security of the system as soon as practicable following discovery, if the personal information was or the entity reasonably believes was accessed and acquired by an unauthorized person.

(d) The notice shall include:

    (1) To the extent possible, a description of the categories of information that were reasonably believed to have been accessed or acquired by an unauthorized person, including social security numbers, driver's licenses, or state identification numbers and financial data;

    (2) A telephone number or website address that the individual may use to contact the entity or the agent of the entity and from whom the individual may learn:

        (A) What types of information the entity maintained about that individual or about individuals in general; and

        (B) Whether or not the entity maintained information about that individual.

    (3) The toll-free contact telephone numbers and addresses for the major credit reporting agencies and information on how to place a fraud alert or security freeze.

(e) Notice required by this section may be delayed if a law-enforcement agency determines and advises the individual or entity that the notice will impede a criminal or civil investigation or homeland or national security. Notice required by this section must be made without unreasonable delay after the law-enforcement agency determines that notification will no longer impede the investigation or jeopardize national or homeland security.

(f) If an entity is required to notify more than one thousand persons of a breach of security pursuant to this article, the entity shall also notify, without unreasonable delay, all consumer reporting agencies that compile and maintain files on a nationwide basis, as defined by 15 U.S.C. §1681a (p), of the timing, distribution and content of the notices. Nothing in this subsection shall be construed to require the entity to provide to the consumer reporting agency the names or other personal identifying information of breach notice recipients. This subsection shall not apply to an entity who is subject to Title V of the Gramm Leach Bliley Act, 15 U.S.C. 6801, *et seq.*

(g) The notice required by this section shall not be considered a debt communication as defined by the Fair Debt Collection Practice Act in 15 U.S.C. §1692a.

§46A-2A-103. Procedures deemed in compliance with security breach notice requirements

(a) An entity that maintains its own notification procedures as part of an information privacy or security policy for the treatment of personal information and that are consistent with the timing requirements of this article shall be deemed to be in compliance with the notification requirements of this article if it notifies residents of this state in accordance with its procedures in the event of a breach of security of the system.

(b) A financial institution that responds in accordance with the notification guidelines prescribed by the Federal Interagency Guidance on Response Programs for Unauthorized Access to Customer Information and Customer Notice is deemed to be in compliance with this article.

(c) An entity that complies with the notification requirements or procedures pursuant to the rules, regulation, procedures, or guidelines established by the entity's primary or functional regulator shall be in compliance with this article.

§46A-2A-104. Violations

(a) Except as provided by subsection (c) of this section, failure to comply with the notice provisions of this article constitutes an unfair or deceptive act of practice in violation of section one hundred four, article six, chapter forty-six-a of this code, which may be enforced by the Attorney General pursuant to the enforcement provisions of this chapter.

(b) Except as provided by subsection (c) of this section, the Attorney General shall have exclusive authority to bring action. No civil penalty may be assessed in an action unless the court finds that the defendant has engaged in a course of repeated and willful violations of this article. No civil penalty shall exceed one hundred fifty thousand dollars per breach of security of the system or series of breaches of a similar nature that are discovered in a single investigation.

(c) A violation of this article by a licensed financial institution shall be enforceable exclusively by the financial institution's primary functional regulator.

§46A-2A-105. Applicability

This article shall apply to the discovery or notification of a breach of the security of the system that occurs on or after the effective date of this article [14].

Notification and mandatory credit protection cost money. Depending on the size of the breach, it could cost millions of dollars to notify all the persons affected. Not reporting the breach could result in criminal and civil penalties. The cost of defending such legal actions would result in even more costs [15].

Notes

[1] Ponemon Cost of Data Breach 2013. http://www.symantec.com/about/news/resources/press_kits/detail.jsp?pkid=ponemon-2013 [accessed on 26.06.13].

[2] HHS.gov: Case Examples and Resolution Agreements. http://www.hhs.gov/ocr/privacy/hipaa/enforcement/examples/index.html [accessed on 26.06.13].

[3] HRSA.gov: What is a "covered entity" under HIPAA? http://www.hrsa.gov/healthit/toolbox/ HealthITAdoptiontoolbox/PrivacyandSecurity/entityhipaa.html [accessed on 26.06.13].

[4] HHS.gov: Security 101 for Covered Entities. http://www.hhs.gov/ocr/privacy/hipaa/ administrative/securityrule/security101.pdf [accessed on 07.07.2013].

[5] OANDP.com: HIPAA Security - Required or Addressable. http://www.oandp.com/articles/ 2003-07_04.asp [accessed on 07.07.2013].

[6] Healthcare Law Blog: MSBCBS of TN Settles HIPAA/HITECH Violation for $1.5M. http:// healthcarebloglaw.blogspot.com/2012/03/msbcbs-of-tn-settles-hipaahitech-breach.html [accessed on 07.07.2013].

[7] Wikipedia: Payment Card Industry Data Security Standard http://en.wikipedia.org/wiki/PCI_ DSS [accessed on 03.07.13].

[8] Boston.com: Cost of data breach at TJX soars to $256m http://www.boston.com/business/ articles/2007/08/15/cost_of_data_breach_at_tjx_soars_to_256m/?page=full [accessed on 03.07.13].

[9] Verizon Data Breach Investigations Report 2012. http://www.verizonbusiness.com/resources/ reports/rp_data-breach-investigations-report-2012_en_xg.pdf [accessed on 08.07.13].

[10] 2011 Cost of Data Breach Study. http://www.symantec.com/content/en/us/about/media/ pdfs/b-ponemon-2011-cost-of-data-breach-us.en-us.pdf?om_ext_cid=biz_socmed_twitter_ facebook_marketwire_linkedin_2012Mar_worldwide__CODB_US [accessed on 08.07.13].

[11] PCI Compliance & Small Merchants: Whose Concern is It Anyway? http://www. pcicomplianceguide.org/merchants-pci-compliance-whose-concern-is-it.php [accessed on 08.07.13].

[12] NCSL: State Security Breach Notification Laws http://www.ncsl.org/issues-research/telecom/ security-breach-notification-laws.aspx [accessed on 03.07.13].

[13] Chapter 46A. West Virginia Consumer Credit and Protection Act. Article 2A. Breach of Security of Consumer Information. http://www.legis.state.wv.us/WVCODE/Code.cfm?chap=46a& art=2A#2A [accessed on 07.07.2013].

[14] State Agency Notice Requirements for Data Breaches Chart. http://www.kelleydrye.com/ publications/articles/1552/_res/id=Files/index=0/State%20Agency%20Notice% 20Requirements%20for%20Data%20Breaches%20Chart%20(5-501-9110)%207%205% 2012.pdf [accessed on 08.07.2013].

[15] Symantec: What can you get for $500,000? Notification for one data breach. http://www. symantec.com/connect/blogs/what-can-you-get-500000-notification-one-data-breach [accessed on 08.07.2013].

CHAPTER 4

Most Attacks Are Targeted

Bill Gardner
Marshall University, Huntington, WV, USA

TARGETED ATTACKS

Most attacks are targeted. They are targeted by either application, port, platform, occupation, or industry. When building an information security awareness program, it is important to include information and examples that are specific to your organization. If your organization is a law firm, point out how bad guys are targeting law firms and lawyers. If your organization is a nonprofit, give examples of how bad guys have targeted nonprofits in the past. These examples go a long way in destroying the myth of "no one wants our stuff."

Attackers target users by targeting applications and services users use daily to do their work and that users use for fun such as social networking. One way attackers target users is through e-mail. Spear phishing attacks take the form of e-mail targeted to a specific user or group of users in enticing the user to click on links contained in the e-mail or to open attachments sent with the e-mail. The first step in crafting a spear phishing e-mail is for the attackers to research their target using your organization's website, social media sites, and other open-source information from online public websites and directories. Once the attackers figure out what the interests of the targeted users are, they will use those interests to build targeted e-mail.

For example, if a targeted user, in this case let's say it's the CEO of an organization, says they are interested in stamp collecting, the attacker will send the targeted user a phishing e-mail about stamp collecting that contains a link or an attachment that will allow the attacker to take control of the targeted user's computer. Once the CEO's computer has been exploited using this method, the attacker will then turn their attention to pivoting the attack to penetrate and exploit the rest of the network and to steal data.

RECENT TARGETED ATTACKS

Attackers recently have begun to target industries related to defense and government contracting. In 2011, RSA, who provides two-factor authentication tokens, called SecurID, to the US government and US government contractors, uncovered a breach of the database that transmits and stores the tokens. During the same period, defense contractors Raytheon, General Dynamics, and L-3 Communications also reported breaches. Some in the industry linked the RSA breach to the other breaches [1]. While some continue to debate if the breaches are somehow linked, they are examples of targeted attacks. Defense contractors hold valuable information from the design of the latest fighter/bomber designs to nuclear research. They definitely hold data that would be valuable to hackers, spies, and other governments.

TARGETED ATTACKS AGAINST LAW FIRMS

In 2009, the FBI alerted law firms and public relations firms that they were being targeted in phishing attacks. The phishing e-mails contained "zip," "jpeg," or other safe-looking attachments that when opened attempt to download and execute the file "srhost.exe" from the domain http://d.ueopen.com. "Law firms have a tremendous concentration of really critical, private information," Bradford Bleier, unit chief in the cyber division of the FBI, told The Associated Press. Infiltrating those computer systems "is a really optimal way to obtain economic, personal and personal security related information" [2].

Beginning in September 2010, Chinese-based hackers broke into law firms based in Canada to derail a $40 billion dollar acquisition of an Australian potash mining company:

> ...hackers rifled one secure computer network after the next, eventually hitting seven different law firms as well as Canada's Finance Ministry and the Treasury Board, according to Daniel Tobok, president of Toronto-based Digital Wyzdom. His cyber security company was hired by the law firms to assist in the probe.
>
> The investigation linked the intrusions to a Chinese effort to scuttle the takeover of Potash Corp. of Saskatchewan Inc. by BHP Billiton Ltd. as part of the global competition for natural resources, Tobok said. Such stolen data can be worth tens of millions of dollars and give the party who possesses it an unfair advantage in deal negotiations, he said.
>
> Though the deal eventually fell apart for unrelated reasons, the incident illustrates the vulnerability of law firms. They are increasingly threatened with a loss of client business if they can't show improved security as such attacks continue to escalate [3].

Typically, the security in law firms has been lower than in other high-profile targets such as banks and other financial institutions. While many lawyers realize they hold sensitive and confidential information on their networks, historically, law firms have not spent time and money to beef up their security to keep attackers from targeting their networks.

According to security firm Mandiant, 80 US-based law firms were breached in 2012. The FBI says as financial firms have become better about information security, law firms are becoming bigger targets. The FBI met with 200 of the top law firms in New York City in the fall of 2011 to engage firms on threat and a rising number of law firm intrusions. The agency warned that "hackers see attorneys as a back door to the valuable data of their corporate clients."

Mary Galligan, head of the cyber division in the New York City office of the FBI at the time, said, "Everybody wants network administrator rights. . .It's trendy." She said partners insist on mobility—including the flexibility to review case documents at weekend homes or on the road—which means highly sensitive documents are routinely transferred by e-mail [4].

In January 2010, the FBI's Internet Crime Complaint Center (IC3) issued a warning about a counterfeit check scheme targeting US law firms:

> The FBI continues to receive reports of counterfeit check scheme targeting U.S. law firms. As previously reported, scammers send e-mails to lawyers, claiming to be overseas and seeking legal representation to collect delinquent payments from third parties in the U.S. The law firm receives a retainer agreement, invoices reflecting the amount owed, and a check payable to the law firm. The firm is instructed to extract the retainer fee, including any other fees associated with the transaction, and wire the remaining funds to banks in Korea, China, Ireland, or Canada. By the time the check is determined to be counterfeit, the funds have already been wired overseas.
>
> In a new twist, the fraudulent client seeking legal representation is an ex-wife "on assignment" in an Asian country, and she claims to be pursuing a collection of divorce settlement monies from her ex-husband in the U.S. The law firm agrees to represent the ex-wife, sends an e-mail to the ex-husband, and receives a "certified" check for the settlement via delivery service. The ex-wife instructs the firm to wire the funds, less the retainer fee, to an overseas bank account. When the scam is executed successfully, the law firm wires the money before discovering the check is counterfeit.
>
> All Internet users need to be cautious when they receive unsolicited e-mails. Law firms are advised to conduct as much due diligence as possible before engaging in transactions with parties who are handling their business solely via e-mail, particularly those parties claiming to reside overseas [5].

In February 2012, Anonymous attacked the law firm of Puckett and Faraj. The DC-based law firm was targeted by the hacktivist group for defending the Marines who killed 24 unarmed Iraqi civilians in Hadith in November 2005. The trial of the Marines ended with an acquittal. Decrying the verdict as unjust, Anonymous launched an assault on the firm's website and internal network that resulted in the defacement of the firm's website and the theft of 2.6 GB of e-mail. The firm's e-mail was later released on Pastebin and Pirate Bay [6].

Even more embarrassing, the firm did not know they had been breached until they were contacted by the website *Gawker*, "Puckett could not be immediately reached for comment; when we called a few minutes ago he was in a meeting and the receptionist had no idea the firm had been hacked" [7]. As of this writing, the firm's website remains off-line nearly two years after the attack [8].

There is no doubt that lawyers and law firms are being targeted (Figure 4.1). Part of defending themselves is to make sure lawyers and staff know the severity and the kinds of threats they face, including spear phishing, to make their data less at risk for social engineering attacks.

OPERATION SHADY RAT

One of the largest examples of a targeted attack is "Operation Shady RAT," which targeted governments, defense contractors, insurance companies, international nonprofits, accounting firms, media outlet, and corporations who specialize in high-technology products and think tanks. According to McAfee, who uncovered the operation, the breaches dated back as far as mid-2006. RAT stands for "remote access tool":

> McAfee won't say who is behind the operation, but it did say that the attacks were organized by one "state actor." Most experts think the hacking sponsor is China. As reported by Reuters, the International Olympic Committee and

FIGURE 4.1 Puckett and Faraj website.

the World Anti-Doping Agency are among the nonprofits that suffered intrusions.

NPQ looked at the McAfee report, which seems to suggest that among the hacking victims were five "international sports" organizations, two think tanks, one "political non-profit," and one "U.S. national security non-profit." Forty-nine of the 72 hacked entities are U.S.-based. These aren't all quick "smash-and-grab" operations. Although some of the intrusions were only one month long, at another, unnamed (Asian) Olympic committee, the hackers were there on and off for 28 months.

McAfee's VP of threat research and author of the McAfee report Dmitri Alperovitch wrote that the firm was "surprised by the enormous diversity of the victim organizations and were taken aback by the audacity of the perpetrators" [9].

The McAfee report also mentions other targeted attacks:

Having investigated intrusions such as Operation Aurora and NightDragon (the systemic long-term compromise of Western oil and gas industry), as well as numerous others that have not been disclosed publicly, I am convinced that every company in every conceivable industry with significant size and valuable intellectual property and trade secrets has been compromised (or will be shortly), with the great majority of the victims rarely discovering the intrusion or its impact. In fact, I divide the entire set of Fortune Global 2000 firms into two categories: those that know they've been compromised and those that don't yet know [10].

McAfee has refused to publicly identify the targets and says that many of the targets refused to believe they had been breached when confronted by the evidence in the McAfee report [10].

OPERATION AURORA

In 2009, Google, Adobe, and a number of other high-profile companies were targeted in an attack that came to be known as Operation Aurora. The attack, which originated out of China, targeted the intellectual property of the target companies, including source code that controlled major systems, including Google's Gmail service. The attackers then used the information gained through the breach to access to the Gmail accounts of human rights activists. "We have never ever, outside of the defense industry, seen commercial industrial companies come under that level of sophisticated attack," says Dmitri Alperovitch, vice president of threat research for McAfee. "It's totally changing the threat model" [11].

NIGHT DRAGON

The Night Dragon attacks, attributed to China, targeted energy corporations. The attacks took place over a four-year period and targeted intellectual property [12]. Also uncovered by McAfee in 2011:

> Starting in November 2009, coordinated covert and targeted cyberattacks have been conducted against global oil, energy, and petrochemical companies. These attacks have involved social engineering, spearphishing attacks, exploitation of Microsoft Windows operating systems vulnerabilities, Microsoft Active Directory compromises, and the use of remote administration tools (RATs) in targeting and harvesting sensitive competitive proprietary operations and project-financing information with regard to oil and gas field bids and operations. We have identified the tools, techniques, and network activities used in these continuing attacks—which we have dubbed Night Dragon—as originating primarily in China [13].

WATERING HOLE ATTACKS

The RSA Advanced Threat Intelligence Team first defined Watering Hole attacks in 2012.

According to RSA, Watering Hole attacks have three phases:

In the new attack we've identified, which we are calling "VOHO," the methodology relies on 'trojanizing' legitimate websites specific to a geographic area which the attacker believes will be visited by end users who belong to the organization they wish to penetrate. This results in a wholesale compromise of multiple hosts inside a corporate network as the end-users go about their daily business, much like a lion will lie in wait to ambush prey at a watering hole.

The details of the attack are still developing, but what we are aware of so far is as follows:

1. The victim visits a compromised 'watering hole' website.
2. This website, through an injected JavaScript element, redirects the visiting browser to an exploit site.
3. This exploit site checks that the visiting machine is running a Windows operating system and a version of Internet Explorer, and then exploits the Java client on the visiting host, installing a 'gh0st RAT' variant [14].

A recent example of a Water Hole or Watering Hole attack is the use of a compromised website containing the menu for a Chinese restaurant to serve exploits to a targeted oil company. The result of the attack was that the attackers were able to circumvent a number of sophisticated defensive measures and products that the company had paid a lot of money to implement.

"Unable to breach the computer network at a big oil company, hackers infected with malware the online menu of a Chinese restaurant that was popular with employees. When the workers browsed the menu, they inadvertently down-loaded code that gave the attackers a foothold in the business's vast computer network" [15].

Watering Hole attacks, while not as popular as phishing attacks, have increased in number over the past few years as users get better at spotting phishing attacks. Watering Hole attacks will likely never pass spear phishing attacks because they require compromising a site that the target regularly uses, which increases the complexity of carrying out the attack. Phishing campaigns are much less com-plex to execute.

COMMON ATTACK VECTORS: COMMON RESULTS

The common attack vectors in Operation Aurora, Operating Shady RAT, and the targeted attacks against RSA and defense contractors where they all used highly targeted spear phishing to infect the organizations with previously unknown malware, which then siphoned confidential information and intel-lectual property out of each organization. The other commonality is that these organizations have spent millions, if not tens of millions, of dollars on antivirus, intrusion detection systems, instruction prevention systems, and other information security defenses and they had been circumvented by someone inside of the organization by simply opening a link or an attach-ment contained in an e-mail, which leads to the compromise of their entire enterprise networks.

All organizations no matter how large or small contain information that is of interest to attackers, and attackers will use any means possible to get to that information. Smaller breaches go unreported because the organization does not know they have been breached or they don't want to admit to business part-ners and customers that they have lost data. The goal of state breach notification laws was to address the part of the problem of underreporting. Just because your organization might be small or midsized doesn't mean that you don't have information of value. In fact, like most organizations, it is likely that your secu-rity program is underbudgeted and understaffed while attackers are well funded and fully staffed by highly trained staff. You are being targeted. Implementing a security awareness program is your best defense against these well-funded, determined attackers.

Notes

[1] DarkReading.com: Targeted Attacks On U.S. Defense Contractors: Fallout From RSA Breach? http://www.darkreading.com/attacks-breaches/targeted-attacks-on-us-defense-contracto/ 229700229 [accessed on 27.07.13].

[2] Law.com: Hackers Targeting Law Firms, FBI Warns. http://legalblogwatch.typepad.com/legal_ blog_watch/2009/11/hackers-targeting-law-firms-fbi-warns.html [accessed on 27.07.13].

[3] Bloomberg: China-Based Hackers Target Law Firms to Get Secret Deal Data. http://www. bloomberg.com/news/2012-01-31/china-based-hackers-target-law-firms.html [accessed on 29.07.13].

[4] Bloomberg: China-Based Hackers Target Law Firms to Get Secret Deal Data. http://www. bloomberg.com/news/2012-01-31/china-based-hackers-target-law-firms.html [accessed on 29.07.13].

[5] Internet Crime and Complaint Center: New Twist on Counterfeit Check Scheme Targeting U.S. Law Firms. http://www.ic3.gov/media/2010/100121.aspx [accessed on 29.07.13].

[6] NMissCommentor: Anonymous targets defense law firm representing Srgt. who led Hadditha Massacre. http://nmisscommentor.com/law/anonymous-targets-defense-law-firm-representing-srgt-who-led-hadditha-massacre/ [accessed on 30.07.13].

[7] Gawker.com: Anonymous Leaks Huge Cache of Emails From Iraq War Crimes Case. http:// gawker.com/5882063/anonymous-releases-huge-cache-of-emails-related-to-iraq-war-crimes-case [accessed on 30.07.13].

[8] http://www.puckettfaraj.com/ [accessed on 30.07.13].

[9] NonProfit Quarterly: Nonprofits Targeted in the World's Biggest Hacking Campaign. http:// www.nonprofitquarterly.org/index.php?option=com_content&view=article&id=14686: nonprofits-targeted-in-the-worlds-biggest-hacking-campaign&catid=155:nonprofit-newswire&Itemid=986 [accessed on 03.08.13].

[10] McAfee: Revealed: Operation Shady RAT. http://www.mcafee.com/us/resources/white-papers/wp-operation-shady-rat.pdf [accessed on 04.08.13].

[11] Wired: ThreatLevel: Google Hack Attack Was Ultra Sophisticated, New Details Show. http:// www.wired.com/threatlevel/2010/01/operation-aurora/ [accessed on 04.08.13].

[12] NetworkWorld: 'Night Dragon' attacks from China strike energy companies. http://www. networkworld.com/news/2011/021011-night-dragon-attacks-from-china.html [accessed on 04.08.13].

[13] McAfee: Global Energy Cyberattacks: "Night Dragon". http://www.mcafee.com/us/resources/ white-papers/wp-global-energy-cyberattacks-night-dragon.pdf [accessed on 04.08.13].

[14] McAfee: Lions at the Watering Hole - The "VOHO" Affair. http://blogs.rsa.com/lions-at-the-watering-hole-the-voho-affair/ [accessed on 04.09.14].

[15] Hackers Lurking in Vents and Soda Machines. http://www.nytimes.com/2014/04/08/ technology/the-spy-in-the-soda-machine.html?_r=0 [accessed on 04.09.14].

CHAPTER 5

Who Is Responsible for Security?

Bill Gardner

Marshall University, Huntington, WV, USA

INFORMATION TECHNOLOGY (IT) STAFF

If asked, most people would say the information technology staff is responsible for securing the data of the organization. This is true because the IT staff is responsible for setting up the servers, network, client computers, firewalls, and other security products located at the edge of the organization's network. They are also likely in charge of installing antivirus software and critical security patches to software and operating systems.

In reality, most IT folks are more concerned with keeping systems up and running than keeping an eye on data security issues. It's the nature of what they do. That's why most organizations rely on security solution hardware and software to keep an eye on data security.

As a result, many IT departments are too overburdened to deal with security in a holistic, proactive approach. As a result, it often ends up at the bottom of the priority list.

The other issue is that keeping systems up and running take a lot of training and technical skill. As a result, the IT team might not be completely up-to-date on what they need to do to secure the organization's data.

It is important not to forget IT when planning and implementing a security awareness program. Help desks are regularly targeted by social engineers in password reset attacks. Unless you give your IT folks the same information and training in regard to security awareness, there might be gaps in their knowledge because assumptions are being made about their level of knowledge of nontechnical attacks such as social engineering, dumpster diving, and phishing.

THE SECURITY TEAM

Some organizations are not large enough to have security teams. If you are lucky enough to have the budget for a security team, they can only guard against known threats. They cannot keep your users from opening attachments and opening links, but they can be an important part of delivering the security awareness message and reminding users of their responsibility to help protect the organizations data.

THE RECEPTIONIST

The receptionist is usually the first line of defense in most organizations. It is the receptionist's job to greet visitors and to direct the visitor or the caller to the correct person to help the customer or visitor in a polite manner. Since the receptionist is likely the first person a visitor sees or the first person they talk to on the phone, the receptionist is the public face of the organization. The duty of the receptionist it to answer questions and to generally provide a good customer service experience. Anything else would reflect poorly on the organization. Social engineers will take advantage of this situation.

Why would a determined attacker spend time and money to steal data by attacking through the firewall when they can just walk in to a company wearing a delivery man's or a telephone repairman's uniform and place data taps on the network or walk out the back door with the company's backup tapes, a computer, or even the organization's server.

Receptionists were never meant to be security guards, yet because of this threat, we have put them in that position. It is very important receptionists receive security awareness training so they understand the unique position they are in, know how to identify social engineering threats, and put in place physical security policies that help them keep your organization safe. These policies include items such as guest/visitor sign-in sheets, guest/visitor badge policies, and guest/visitor escort policies.

THE CEO

The CEO has access to everything on the organization's network. The CEO is also a busy person whose top priority is to make sure the organization is running efficiently and with an eye on the bottom line. The CEO has a huge target on their back. Attackers would love to gain access or steal the CEO or other key manager's computer or laptop.

Management is often the hardest to get to security awareness training events. As a result, it is important to remember to find alternative forms of delivery for security awareness training and reminders for the CEO and other management types.

ACCOUNTING

If an attacker is interested in money, they are going to launch a spear phishing attack against the organization's accounting department. On security assessments and penetration tests, it is shocking how little thought goes into securing the part of the organization whose mission is to handle money. It is not uncommon to find passwords, bank account log-in information, and wire transfer information kept in text documents, unencrypted and without password protection on the desktops of accounting employees. One successful spear phishing attempt would put the attacker in a position to empty the organization's bank accounts.

THE MAILROOM/COPY CENTER

The mailroom/copy center needs to use computers just as much as anyone else. In fact, a large amount of information, which can include financial data and medical records, are stored on their computer for copying and mailing jobs. As a result, these roles need to be included in security awareness training as well.

THE RUNNER/COURIER

These are the people who have charge of the organization's backup data while it's being taken to off-site storage. Do they know how to keep the tapes or other media in sight at all times? What if they leave it on a desk during a delivery to another location? What if they leave them in the delivery vehicle and they are stolen? These are huge risks to an organization's data that need to be addressed. As a result, these folks need to be included in the security awareness training.

EVERYONE IS RESPONSIBLE FOR SECURITY

Users by the nature of their job duties inherit certain risks. Treating everyone the same, regardless of education level or user role, is a huge mistake. Highly educated professionals such as doctors, lawyers, accountants, and college professors can be the hardest groups to target for security awareness training because they feel their years of education have made them immune to social engineering tricks. Yet many of these professionals, especially lawyers, are being targeted because security programs and security awareness programs have been overlooked as a priority.

In recent years, Chinese hackers have targeted Toronto's Bay Street law firm to derail a $40 billion acquisition of the world's largest potash producer [1]. In November 2013, a Pittsburgh man was sentenced for "recklessly damaging a computer and password trafficking" in a case that involved a law firm's computer system [2]. As late as 2012, the FBI has warned lawyers that their firms need to increase their security because they were being targeted [3].

It's not just lawyers, accountants are being targeted as well [4]. Many professional organizations are repositories of confidential information, thus becoming targets. In May 2014, the Justice Department issued a 31-count indictment of five Chinese military officers for breaking into the networks of six American corporations to steal intellectual property. The data were worth billions of dollars accounting to the indictments.

> "For years the Chinese—especially, but not exclusively, a Shanghai-based department of the People's Liberation Army called Unit 61398 (where all of the indicted officers work)—have been hacking into the computer networks of U.S. corporations, defense firms, and financial institutions. President Obama and a few Cabinet secretaries have raised the issue in several diplomatic forums. Each time, Chinese officials have denied the charges and challenged the Americans to produce some evidence. The indictment is, in this sense, the reply: Here is the evidence—and in staggering detail" [5].

Threats such as Chinese hackers and industrial espionage do not ring true with all employees of an organization. The mailroom staff, secretaries, and receptionist, for example, have very little concept of what industrial espionage or intellectual property is, let alone how to protect it. As a result, attackers will use this knowledge gap in the form of phishing, infected attachments, and other social engineering to exploit these users and then pivot their attacks to steal the data they are after. We have already made receptionist security guards; now we make mailroom staff, secretaries, and other support staff network defenders through an effective security awareness program.

With the proliferation of social media sites and the proliferation of social engineering attacks and scams on social media, the risk is more than just clicking links in e-mail and opening the wrong attachment. There is also the risk that the confidential and privileged information that might aid an attacker might be posted to social media. Many users pick passwords based on information such as their pet's name, their spouse's name, their birth date, or other information that an attacker can find on social media. Users can also unintentionally reveal operational details of the organization such as the location of branch offices or the type of antivirus software installed on the organization's computers. While most people think of the traditional sites for social networking such as Twitter and Facebook, there are literally hundreds of social networking sites that users might be using [6,7]. In the case of LinkedIn, the service actually caters to business networking. Beyond data leakage, these sites can house malware. Since anyone can typically upload any code they want to these sites, social media sites have been the points of infections for zero days in the past [8]. With the prevalent use of social media in originations at all levels, informing users of the threats that exist on social media platforms and how to detect and avoid them is especially important.

In the case of midlevel managers and at higher levels in the organization, it can be useful to point out the financial harm a data breach can cause an organization. The recent breach at Target shows how a company can suffer financially and how repercussions can extend to people losing their jobs [9]. No one wants to be involved in a resume-generating event. Target has experienced a large amount of financial pain that has been directly linked to the breach from low earnings to the cost of ongoing litigation related to the breach [10,11]. The Target breach is remarkable because it is the first clear-cut and well-publicized case of a retailer suffering large financial losses as a result of the credit card breach. During the TJX breach in 2007, the stock actually rose after initial losses, and the stock has continued to do well over time. TJX remains one of the largest breaches in history [12,13].

In the case of employees, it is important to emphasize the amount of personal information the organization collects about them in order to pay them and provide them and their dependents with medical and other insurances. When risk is made personal, more people will take notice of the importance of securing the organization's data because it has now been explained how a breach could also affect their personal data. People check their bank accounts from work, shop from work, and have pictures of their loved ones stored on their computer. How would they feel if the flight reservations of their college-aged daughter ended up in the wrong hands?

When risks and the consequences of a breach are personalized, compliance with policies that keeps information safe will increase. No matter what our position in our respective organizations, we are all network defenders.

Notes

[1] China-Based Hackers Target Law Firms to Get Secret Deal Data. http://www.bloomberg.com/news/2012-01-31/china-based-hackers-target-law-firms.html [accessed on 22.05.2014].

[2] Pittsburgh Man Sentenced for Role in Law Firm Hack. http://www.fbi.gov/pittsburgh/press-releases/2013/pittsburgh-man-sentenced-for-role-in-law-firm-hack [accessed on 22.05.2014].

[3] China-Based Hackers Target Law Firms to Get Secret Deal Data. http://www.bloomberg.com/news/2012-01-31/china-based-hackers-target-law-firms.html [accessed on 23.05.2014].

[4] Security Issues for Accountants. http://www.lagfoa.org/Security-Issues-for-Accountants.pdf [accessed on 23.05.2014].

[5] Why Did the Justice Department Indict Five Chinese Military Officers? http://www.slate.com/articles/news_and_politics/war_stories/2014/05/justice_department_indicts_five_chinese_military_officers_can_the_obama.html [accessed on 23.05.2014].

[6] Beyond Facebook: 74 Popular Social Networks Worldwide http://www.practicalecommerce.com/articles/2701-Beyond-Facebook-74-Popular-Social-Networks-Worldwide [accessed on 26.05.2014].

[7] List of social networking websites http://en.wikipedia.org/wiki/List_of_social_networking_websites [accessed on 26.05.2014].

[8] Details Emerge On Latest Adobe Flash Zero-Day Exploit http://threatpost.com/details-emerge-on-latest-adobe-flash-zero-day-exploit/104068 [accessed on 26.05.2014].

[9] Target CIO resigns following breach. http://www.computerworld.com/s/article/9246773/Target_CIO_resigns_following_breach [accessed on 24.05.2014].

[10] Target Earnings Show Pain of Data Breach Is Far From Over http://www.businessweek.com/articles/2014-05-21/target-earnings-show-pain-of-data-breach-is-far-from-over [accessed on 26.05.2014].

[11] Target Faces Nearly 70 Lawsuits Over Breach http://blogs.wsj.com/riskandcompliance/2014/01/15/target-faces-nearly-70-lawsuits-over-breach/ [accessed on 24.05.2014].

[12] Giant Retailer Reveals Customer Data Breach http://online.wsj.com/news/articles/SB116906153282079233 [accessed on 24.05.2014].

[13] Yahoo Finance: TJX Stock Chart http://finance.yahoo.com/echarts?s=TJX+Interactive#symbol=TJX;range=my [accessed on 24.05.2014].

CHAPTER 6

Why Current Programs Don't Work

Bill Gardner
Marshall University, Huntington, WV, USA

THE LECTURE IS DEAD AS A TEACHING TOOL

No one likes a lecture, except maybe the person giving it. For the lecturer, the act of giving a lecture is an active exercise. For those attending, the lecture is a passive exercise. Passive learning is shown to be not as effective as active learning when conveying information. In fact, many in higher education say that the lecture, a centuries-old teaching technique, is dead [1].

Research shows that we should do something that universities have been moving toward in the past few years: replacing passive learning with active learning. Active learning depending on how it is implemented has become known at "peer instruction" or "interactive learning." These techniques make the student responsible for their own learning as well as fostering interaction with other students in interacting with the material to be learned [2].

"Peer instruction" and "interactive learning" take the form of giving students assignments to read or videos to watch and then splitting the students into groups to interact with the material. These interactions involve writing assignments, group discussion, completing assigned tasks as a team, and sometimes a group grade [3]. Sometimes, students play question and answer games based on popular game show formats to engage the material. Points can be awarded in candy or toward a group grade [4].

We know that what we are doing now isn't working because we see examples of breaches that involved exploiting a human in order to gain access to data on an almost daily basis. Users are also showing signs of message malaise. Most users think they will never be tricked into clicking on a link or opening an attachment, because they view themselves as savvy Internet users.

Bruce Schneier, chief security technology officer at BT, wrote an opinion piece for the website Darkreading.com in March 2013 saying that money spent on user awareness training would be better spent on better system design [5]. The post caused a firestorm in information security circles. Some people agree with him but most do not [6,7]. Everybody agrees we have to do something, even Schneier says, "Security is a process, not a product" [8]. If we never inform end users of threats, they will never know about them.

Security awareness has a lot in common with other awareness campaigns. Other awareness campaigns use memorable spokesmen like Smokey the Bear and McGruff the Crime Dog. They also have memorable slogans like "Only you can prevent forest fires," and "Take a bite out of crime." In the field of information security awareness, we fail at these two simple goals because we continue to have debates about the effectiveness of security awareness programs.

As Bruce Schneier says, "Security is a process, and not a product" [8]. The process of security is a long hard road that begins with getting management buy-in, drafting and enforcing policies that give the user expectations of what they can and cannot do with the organizations technological resources, building an effective security awareness program, and then measuring the effectiveness of that program using meaningful metrics.

Once metrics are gathered and processed, the cycle begins again with a review of policies, awareness program, and metrics, and changes are made based on the organization's needs.

Doing something is better than doing nothing. The main purpose behind this book is to give people the tools to do something rather than nothing. While there is value in making sure your organization has the latest security products and that your IT staff has proper security training, it is a waste of time and money if you ignore the human factor. Next-generation firewalls, antivirus, intrusion detection systems, intrusion prevention systems, and web application firewalls are all great productions, but these products do not provide protection against an employee making a poor decision about clicking links, opening attachments, and other nontechnical attacks employed by social engineers.

People have different learning styles based upon generational and educational background. The current generation currently entering the workforce learns much differently than those entering the workforce thirty years ago. Some people learn better from reading, others are visual learners, and some learn best from listening.

The Seven Learning Styles

- **Visual (spatial):** You prefer using pictures, images, and spatial understanding.
- **Aural (auditory-musical):** You prefer using sound and music.
- **Verbal (linguistic):** You prefer using words, in both speech and writing.

- **Physical (kinesthetic):** You prefer using your body, hands, and sense of touch.
- **Logical (mathematical):** You prefer using logic, reasoning, and systems.
- **Social (interpersonal):** You prefer to learn in groups or with other people.
- **Solitary (intrapersonal):** You prefer to work alone and use self-study.

Why Learning Styles? Understand the basis of learning styles

Your learning styles have more influence than you may realize. Your preferred styles guide the way you learn. They also change the way you internally represent experiences, the way you recall information, and even the words you choose. We explore more of these features in this chapter.

Research shows us that each learning style uses different parts of the brain. By involving more of the brain during learning, we remember more of what we learn. Researchers using brain imaging technologies have been able to find out the key areas of the brain responsible for each learning style.

For example:

- **Visual:** The occipital lobes at the back of the brain manage the visual sense. Both the occipital and parietal lobes manage spatial orientation.
- **Aural:** The temporal lobes handle aural content. The right temporal lobe is especially important for music.
- **Verbal:** The temporal and frontal lobes, especially two specialized areas called the Broca and Wernicke areas (in the left hemisphere of these two lobes).
- **Physical:** The cerebellum and the motor cortex (at the back of the frontal lobe) handle much of our physical movement.
- **Logical:** The parietal lobes, especially the left side, drive our logical thinking.
- **Social:** The frontal and temporal lobes handle much of our social activities. The limbic system (not shown apart from the hippocampus) also influences both the social and solitary styles. The limbic system has a lot to do with emotions, moods, and aggression.
- **Solitary:** The frontal and parietal lobes, and the limbic system, are also active with this style [9].

The best strategy is to teach to a mixture of learning styles to see what works best for your organization. Studies have shown that hands-on learning is retained more than other kinds of learning [10,11]. Hands-on learning is active learning. Traditional security awareness programs are composed of slide shows, lectures, and videos. If the slide shows, lectures, and videos are given in person rather than delivered via a website, it is a step toward more active learning since it gives opportunities for the trainer and the participants to interact.

"Active learning" is defined as "... an approach to classroom instruction in which students engage material through talking, writing, reading, reflecting, or questioning—in other words, through being active." Active learning puts aside the old practices of simply lecturing employees on security best practices. The approach takes security awareness program to the next level through exercises involving talking, reading, writing, reflecting, and questioning [12].

For example, instead of telling users what a good password policy is, ask them if they can explain the best practices for passwords and discuss what makes a good password. Another example is for trainees to discuss the types of malware they have encountered in the past, how they think it got on their computers, and what they think the attacker was after. This will help to illustrate to users that malware isn't just an inconvenience that slows down their computer, but is an attempt by online criminals to steal data off of their computers, to use their computer as part of a botnet, to use their computer to hide child porn and other contraband, or to use their computer to gain a beachhead to further their attack on the organization's network and steal more data. Both of these examples involve discussion but both could make a good writing and discussion exercise if you ask them to write down their answers and then discuss them. Another exercise would be to have the trainees to read one or more of the organization's security policies and then to reflect on why the policy is in place and to question why the organization needs such a policy.

As you can see, this can be a process that takes more than a few minutes when an employee starts or an hour during the yearly security awareness day. Active learning exercises will require an organization to implement a continuous learning paradigm (Figure 6.1). One personal example of this is the reminder cards I left on people's desks when they did not lock their computer screens.

While users found the reminder intrusive, over time, we had people become more compliant with the policy. Security awareness programs will become more effective if organizations place more time, money, and value in them. Once a year is not enough. A quick look at the news of continuing breaches because of social engineering attacks or a quick look at http://www.ponemon.org/ at

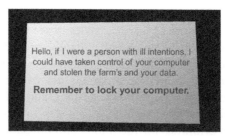

FIGURE 6.1 Screen locking reminder card.

the ongoing costs of data breaches should be enough to illustrate that while security awareness programs are getting better, we are not doing enough. Organizations spend millions of dollars a year on security products to protect their network edge. Organizations also need to start giving time and money to security awareness programs to protect themselves, their business partners, and their customers from social engineering attacks.

Building a security awareness program is a process. The most important thing one can do is to begin that process with the end in mind. No organization will be totally secure and no security awareness program will completely protect you from breaches. Breaches will still happen, but with the right amount of effort, you can make your organization more secure and hopefully less likely to suffer a breach from social engineering.

Notes

[1] Is the Lecture Dead? http://www.theatlantic.com/health/archive/2013/01/is-the-lecture-dead/272578/ [accessed on 24.10.2013].

[2] Twilight of the Lecture. http://harvardmagazine.com/2012/03/twilight-of-the-lecture [accessed on 24.10.2013].

[3] The Physics Suite: Peer Instruction Problems. http://www.physics.umd.edu/perg/role/PIProbs/ [accessed on 24.10.2013].

[4] How to Ignite Peer to Peer learning with Games http://www.quora.com/Michelle-Jaramilla/Posts/How-to-Ignite-Peer-to-Peer-Learning-with-GamesHow-to-Ignite-Peer-to-Peer-Learning-with-Games [accessed on 24.10.2013].

[5] On Security Awareness Training http://www.darkreading.com/hacked-off/on-security-awareness-training/240151108 [accessed on 29.11.2013].

[6] Does Security Awareness Training Actually Improve Enterprise Security http://www.safelightsecurity.com/does-security-awareness-training-actually-improve-enterprise-security/ [accessed on 29.11.2013].

[7] The Debate on Security Education and Awareness https://www.trustedsec.com/march-2013/the-debate-on-security-education-and-awareness/ [accessed on 29.11.2013].

[8] The Process of Security https://www.schneier.com/essay-062.html [accessed on 29.11.2013].

[9] Overview of Learning Styles http://www.learning-styles-online.com/overview/ [accessed on 24.05.2014].

[10] The use of learning style innovations to improve retention http://ieeexplore.ieee.org/xpl/login.jsp?tp=&arnumber=483166&url=http%3A%2F%2Fieeexplore.ieee.org%2Fxpls%2Fabs_all.jsp%3Farnumber%3D483166 [accessed on 24.05.2014].

[11] Do Hands-On, Technology-Based Activities Enhance Learning by Reinforcing Cognitive Knowledge and Retention? http://files.eric.ed.gov/fulltext/EJ458788.pdf [accessed on 24.05.2014].

[12] University of Minnesota Center for Teaching and Learning http://www1.umn.edu/ohr/teachlearn/tutorials/active/ [accessed on 24.05.2014].

CHAPTER 7

Social Engineering

Valerie Thomas
Securicon, Lorton, VA, USA

WHAT IS SOCIAL ENGINEERING?

"Nice weather we're having," Mark said with a grin as he flicked his lighter to the cigarette in his mouth while struggling to hold his umbrella. "Yeah, just great," agreed Jerry as he blew out a cloud of smoke toward the windows of an office building. Taking another drag, Jerry asked, "Did you catch the game last night?" Mark flicked some ashes to the ground, "Nah, the wife wanted to check out some new tapas place. Spent 70 bucks and I'm still hungry." Jerry smirked as the two men extinguished their smokes. "Yeah, I know how that goes," he said with a nod as Mark swiped his access card and held the door as Jerry shook the rain from his jacket and then stepped inside the building. The men went opposite ways in the hallway. Mark returned to his desk to take an incoming call. Jerry found an empty conference room to set up his laptop and then began stealing the company's data.

You see, Jerry wasn't an employee; he was an attacker.

Social engineering is the art of gaining trust or acceptance in order to persuade someone to provide information or perform an action to benefit the attacker. Even though most social engineering attacks are nontechnical, when combined with technical attacks, the results can be disastrous for the target. Famous hacker Kevin Mitnick coined the term social engineering in his first book The Art of Deception. Using persuasion and deception in combination with technical attacks, Mitnick was able to infiltrate organizations such as Pacific Bell and Nortel before his apprehension in 1995. Upon his release in 2000, Mitnick founded Mitnick Security Consulting and is now one of the most sought-after computer experts in the world.

WHO ARE SOCIAL ENGINEERS?

Not all hackers fit the stereotype of an antisocial teenager living in his mom's basement; the same applies to social engineers. Most social engineers are highly extroverted and have no qualms about chatting up a stranger. In order to manipulate the trust of people, one must be willing to talk to them. Usually, they dress to blend into the environment but occasionally dress to stand out if the situation is right. It also isn't safe to assume that all social engineers and hackers are men. Women are perceived to be less threatening than men, which enable them to be very effective attackers. Above all, they are likeable people who make others they come in contact with feel good about them.

WHY DOES IT WORK?

From a young age, we're taught "The Golden Rule: Treat others the way you want to be treated." When we see someone struggling, our first reaction is to help him or her. This is especially true if the person indicates that he or she will get in trouble if the target doesn't help. Social engineering uses our psychological makeup against us by striving for empathy from the target. Empathy is the drive to identify another person's emotions and/or thoughts and respond with the appropriate emotion. Lastly, these types of attacks are effective because many people are unaware of what social engineering attacks are and the threat they pose.

HOW DOES IT WORK?

Not all social engineering attacks are designed to yield pieces of sensitive information, such as passwords. Some are meant to obtain a piece of information that seems insignificant to the target, such as the name of their cleaning company. The attacker uses these smaller pieces of information to create a cover story, or pretext, to perform an attack. The goal of a pretext is to pass the age-old "Duck Test: If it looks like a duck, swims like a duck, and quacks like a duck, then it probably is a duck."

The attack cycle can be broken into three phases:

- Information gathering
- Attack planning
- Attack execution

For the sake of discussion, we'll combine attack planning and execution, as we'll site many examples and don't want to confuse them.

INFORMATION GATHERING

Deception is a very meticulous business that involves the smallest of details, in some cases including the weather. In order for a social engineer to be successful, they have to blend into the target environment.

Blending isn't merely physical; one must also be able to speak the lingo of the organization and know its key players. Information is gathered from a multitude of Internet sources. We'll discuss the most popular resources and how a social engineer uses them.

The Company Website

Social engineers examine the target's website closely for some obvious reasons, such as identifying their industry and products/services. Some less obvious items they look for are the following:

- Number of employees—It's more difficult to social engineer an organization where everyone is on a first-name basis, difficult but not impossible.
- Locations—Understanding where the target's offices are located is crucial. If the attacker is going to impersonate an employee from engineering, they want to be sure that their target is not sitting in the next cubicle.
- Job openings—Detailed postings provide insight into specific technologies that the target may be using, such as antivirus and intrusion detection systems (IDS). Job postings also provide high-level detail on where company departments are located. For example, three accounting jobs are posted with a location of Dallas.
- Names of executives and managers—This information can be used to draft an organizational chart.
- E-mail address format—Once an attacker knows the target's e-mail scheme, such as john.smith@abc.com, they can create e-mail lists with names discovered from other sources. The user's naming scheme in their e-mail address can sometimes be the same format for their login username.
- Current events—Has the target company merged with another company recently? Posing as an employee from the newly acquired company could be a possible attack vector. Are they having any events that are open to the public? These events can be an opportunity to learn company lingo and observe their level of security awareness.

Ultimately, attackers need a granular understanding of the target in order to pose as an employee or trusted insider. The company website is a valuable intelligence source, but not the only one.

Social Media

While social media websites are great for staying connected with friends and colleagues, they are fertile hunting ground for attackers. Facebook and Twitter provide an in-depth look into the personal lives of potential targets. In addition to a near real-time update of the person's activities, other pieces of useful information are usually included. A few examples include

- names of family members
- high school attended
- birthday
- names of pets
- favorite color
- hobbies or interests

All the items listed above provide potential answers to password reset or other security-related questions. These pieces of personal information also provide an attacker potential attack vectors for infecting the victim's computer, more about that later.

To a social engineer, LinkedIn is a shopping list for targets. The granular search options allow for filters such as current employer, previous employer, physical location, industry, and more. Want to know who works in the engineering department of your target company? No problem. With a premium LinkedIn account and a few tailored searches, you can have a list in a matter of minutes. Better yet, most profiles include a partial resume detailing job duties and technical skills, which provide an overview of defensive technologies in place at the target organization.

Search Engines

Using your search engine of choice, it may be possible to obtain "juicy" documents. These may obtain internal information such as common acronyms, financial details, network diagrams, and other items of interest. Some refer to this as "Google hacking," but any search engine will suffice. The following examples are written for Google searching:

- "Company name" internal filetype:doc
- "Company name" sensitive filetype:xls
- "Company name" private filetype:ppt
- "Company name" "do not disseminate" filetype:pdf

The Dumpster

Dumpster diving is an old and popular information gathering method. Although it isn't very enjoyable, it often yields great results. During red team assessments, my team has discovered everything from documents marked "Sensitive-Do Not Print" to ID cards that opened the facility door. You'd be surprised just how much information the dumpster may hold…just don't forget to wear gloves.

The Popular Lunch Spot

Ever heard the phrase "Loose lips sink ships?" Often times, if an attacker (or anyone else for that matter) wants to know what's going on in an organization, all they need to do is go to lunch. Hitting the popular restaurants and cafes around the target location is a no-risk method for gathering data. If two or more coworkers are together for any length of time, it's almost inevitable that they will "talk shop." The larger the group, the more detailed the conversation. When I train security professionals in the ways of social engineering, one of their assignments is to go out to lunch and do nothing but listen to conversations around them and take notes. There's usually a prize waiting for whoever brings back the juiciest story. The next time you're in a restaurant or coffee shop, try it for yourself and see what knowledge can be gained by simply listening. Employees of the target company are usually easy to spot based on the forgotten ID card dangling from their neck or corporate shirts and jackets. This is also a fantastic opportunity to learn company lingo.

ATTACK PLANNING AND EXECUTION

Jerry the Attacker

Let's revisit our characters from the beginning of the chapter. Prior to arriving onsite, Jerry had gathered multiple aerial maps of the target location in an attempt to locate potential smoking areas. Generally, smoking areas are in the side or back of the building away from the main entrance and away from most security guards. Once Jerry arrived onsite, he had an early lunch at a café across the street and observed the building from a distance. As the waiter served his burger and fries, Jerry spotted Mark in the smoking area along with two other men. Jerry recognized Mark from his LinkedIn profile picture, which reaffirmed the target location was correct. Popping a few fries into his mouth, he watched as the men made conversation and then smiled as Mark held the door open for everyone heading back inside as the rain began to fall.

While the above example appears simple and straightforward, a significant amount of time was invested researching potential attack vectors for the target company. Not only did Jerry need a plan to obtain building access, but also he needed to plan his goals once inside, and an exit strategy if detected.

The Spear Phishing E-mail

During the information gathering phase, the attackers discovered that their target company was using a Cisco VPN client. Employees were able to install the client on their work laptops to connect to the corporate network upon proper authentication. The attackers then created a malicious version of the VPN client software that would provide them with access to the victim's computer but would still function as a normal VPN client. Once the malicious VPN client was fully functional, the attackers performed the following actions to carry out the attack:

- Purchased a domain similar to the target company's.
- Selected the target employee by reviewing the gathered names and job titles. They selected "Dan" from the marketing department who traveled frequently (and was therefore very dependent on the VPN). Dan was also selected because of his nontechnical position in the company. Nontechnical employees are less likely to question a coworker from the company's network team when instructed to install software.
- Selected the employee whose name they would use to send the attack e-mail. According to his LinkedIn profile, Joey was the lead network engineer for the company. Choosing a person with seniority is preferred because people are more likely to comply with a request from an authoritative figure, rather than a low- or mid-level employee.
- Configured an e-mail address for Joey at their newly purchased domain.
- Then, they waited. Remember, in social engineering attacks, timing is everything. They waited until Joey had announced on Twitter that he would be attending a conference for the remainder of the week out of state.
- Late Friday morning, the attackers e-mailed Dan from Joey's fictitious account stating:
  "In order to increase connection speed and availability we have upgraded the VPN Infrastructure. A client software update is required for use. Users who do not update by COB today will no longer have VPN access.
  All VPN users must update their client software by running the attached installation program.
  A system restart is not required. Please contact User Support if additional assistance is required."
  Respectfully,
  Joey Smith
  Network Operations
  Ext. 1402
- The team monitored the fictitious e-mail account for activity. A few minutes later, Dan replied saying that he had installed the software. The attackers then had obtained full access to Dan's system and the company network.

It may seem unrealistic that an attacker would spend weeks researching and preparing for an attack just to send a single e-mail, but this is a prime example of a real-world social engineering attack. Taking small pieces of data from multiple sources and creating a believable story is what social engineering is all about. Another view into this is that a few short weeks of intelligence gathering, one e-mail, and one piece of software have thwarted hundreds of thousands of dollars of a company's security infrastructure.

Hello, Help Desk?

Sarah was targeting a large insurance company with offices throughout the United States. Locating their web-based e-mail and VPN sites had been trivial with some customized search terms. The websites didn't require certificate-based authentication, and from what Sarah could tell without valid login credentials, two-factor authentication was not in place. This meant that all she needed was a valid username and password to access the company's resources. Using the tool FOCA, Sarah examined the metadata in various documents and presentations located on the company website. The metadata search yielded ten usernames using the scheme first initial and last name. Now that Sarah understood the username format, she could easily deduce usernames with only the employee's name. Then Sarah searched Facebook for employees of the target company and discovered 43. Of those 43 profiles, 20 of them were completely open to the public. Open profiles reveal all data that have been entered into Facebook, including the user's status updates. Sarah compiled a list of female employees with open Facebook profiles and began searching for additional information, such as signature blocks and office phone numbers.

It was the week of Christmas and the holiday season was in full swing. Sarah monitored the list of female employees with open Facebook profiles until the right status update appeared from Natalie Green. "Heading to Hawaii for ten blissful days away from the snow and ice!" This was great news for Sarah! Now, Sarah could attempt to gain control over Natalie's account with little risk of detection. Sarah compiled her list of notes on Natalie including birthday, hometown, office and cell phone numbers, home address, department name, work title, and supervisor name.

On Christmas Eve at 7:00 PM, Sarah contacted the help desk using a caller ID spoofing program to make her number appear as Natalie's cell phone. A pleasant-sounding young man answered. "Help desk, this is Paul. How may I help you?" Using her best "whiny voice," Sarah replied. "Hi Paul. This is Natalie Green from the Denver office. I changed my password earlier this week, and now I can't remember it. It wouldn't be such a big deal if I wasn't on call this week." She said with a sigh. Paul gave a knowing chuckle "Understand that all too well. Let's get you back online Natalie. I just need your office phone number to verify your identity." Sarah blinked in surprise. Could it really be this easy? She bit her tongue to hold back the excitement. "Sure thing, Paul." She replied and proceeded to read the phone number from her notes. The line went quiet, but Sarah could hear typing and the low melody of Christmas music in the background. "You're all set, Natalie. I set your password to '2013Denver$,' but you'll have to change it once you log in." Sarah smiled and let out an audible sigh of relief. "Thanks a lot Paul. I really appreciate your help tonight. I hope you aren't stuck there tomorrow too." Paul replied "Thankfully no, but I'll be here the rest of the night if you run into any more problems." Sarah began typing in Natalie's username and new password to verify they were in working order. "Looks like I'm good to go. Thanks again Paul. Have a Merry Christmas!" Sarah now had unrestricted access to Natalie's account for the entire week. Prior to Natalie's scheduled return, Sarah installed a backdoor that would allow her access into Natalie's account even after her password had been changed.

Help desks are prime targets for attackers because their entire purpose is to help people. The attack was performed on the evening of a holiday due to the high probability that a less experienced employee would be on shift. This was a fail-safe in case Sarah was missing a piece of key information to verify her identity. The new employee would be more likely to break procedure in order to help keep someone out of trouble.

THE SOCIAL ENGINEERING DEFENSIVE FRAMEWORK (SEDF)

As a security consultant, I've performed social engineering assessments for a multitude of clients—from e-commerce to government and everything in between. Each engagement is unique, but almost always results in the same question from management: "How do we stop social engineering attacks?" I found that I didn't have a definitive resource to refer them to or even a high-level guideline to get them started.

The simple truth is that social engineering attacks can't be stopped with technology alone, nor can they be stopped with training alone. I created the Social Engineering Defensive Framework (SEDF) to help organizations prevent social engineering attacks at the enterprise level. SEDF outlines basic phases for attack prevention:

- Determine exposure
- Evaluate defenses
- Educate the workforce
- Streamline existing technology and policy

The SEDF phases are independent from each other and can be performed in an order that suits the priorities of the organization. If you've just completed a large training campaign, then perhaps evaluating defense is the next step for you.

Determine Exposure

This phase focuses on seeing websites and other available resources through the eyes of a social engineer. A web exposure assessment is a nonintrusive method of gathering client information in order to provide a clear picture on what data are exposed to the Internet.

A major area of focus is the company website. Are you providing too much information? An online employee directory, while helpful to customers, is a gold mine for social engineers. In most cases, listing key customer-focused employees provides customers with the point of contact without listing every-one who works at the company. Superfluous job postings can provide details about software deployed in your environment. Announcing your brand of anti-virus and other deployed security technologies to the world is like putting out the welcome mat for attackers. Metadata analysis is a key part of the assessment to determine if usernames, passwords, and operating system details are exposed in documents that are posted on your website.

Another portion of the assessment is searching for leaked documents. Not all of these documents are discovered via Google. Peer-to-peer networks, social media, and other information-sharing websites can be excellent resources. Whenever I perform one of these assessments and attach the discovered documents, the client always asks, "Where did you get this!?"

A few other areas of focus are the following:

- Technical support forums—You'd be surprised how many folks register for these using their company e-mail address. Code snippets and file paths can be very helpful when planning a technical attack.
- Social media—These resources provide insight into the lives of employees and are fertile hunting ground for attackers. Personal details such as what high school they attended or pet names are often used as password reset questions. Also, knowing if someone is going to be on vacation for a week provides an attacker the opportunity to masquerade as that employee with minimal risk of detection.
- Popular hacking websites—Websites similar to http://pastebin.com are popular dumping ground for attackers and can contain everything from account data to intellectual property.

Once the research is complete, a report is made summarizing the discovered information and the most likely attack vectors. In addition to listing attack vectors, include recommendations on how to reduce exposure of the discovered data.

Evaluate Defenses

This phase can be utilized to evaluate employee resistance and reaction to simulated attacks. Organizations can also elect to evaluate the effectiveness of detection technology and appropriate response groups. Types of simulated attacks include phishing, phone, and physical. It is common practice to outsource these assessments to a specialized vendor, but is not required.

Phishing assessments evaluate the organization's resistance against malicious e-mail content. Content can vary from hyperlinks, attachments, to HTML forms to harvest employee information or gain access to their computer. Phishing attacks are popular with attackers and should be high on the list of your organization's cyber threats. If your organization has not performed this type of assessment, a simulated phishing attack should be the first evaluated defense in this process. The detailed process for creating simulated phishing attacks can be found in Chapter 10.

Phone attacks, otherwise known as vishing, trick individuals into divulging information via a phone call or text message. Attackers perform caller ID spoofing, which causes their call to appear to be from a known phone number. Caller ID spoofing is not illegal in the United States and can be performed using a commercial service or with personal equipment. While vishing may seem out of date, it is still an extremely useful tool for attackers because their targets don't have time to think the situation through prior to providing information to the attacker. Focus your initial simulated phone attacks against employees that mainly deal with the public. Help desk personnel, sales, public relations, and human resources should be included in the initial evaluation.

Physical security education is often overlooked in awareness programs. Although physical security and cyber security usually report to different departments, they are both working to protect the same assets. Completing a physical security assessment can be an eye-opening experience for both physical and cyber security. Physical penetration tests evaluate security controls by gaining access to a specified facility or room. Team members often exploit electronic controls and utilize social engineering to obtain access. Often, physical security assessments are performed in conjunction with a network penetration test. Physical security basics and assessments are covered in detail in Chapter 8.

This outcome of this phase should answer the following questions:

Employees
- Was access or information obtained?
  - Workstation
  - Server
  - Physical
- How many employees provided information or access?
- What weaknesses or vulnerabilities were utilized to obtain information or access?
  - Technology
  - Human
  - Physical barriers, such as fences
- How many employees reported suspicious activity?
  - Correctly
  - Incorrectly

Defenders
- How many attacks were detected?
- What was the average detection time?
- How were attacks detected?
  - Employee reported suspicious activity
  - Technical alert from IDS/antivirus/proxy
  - Alert from security camera or access control system
  - Discovered by guard force while on patrol
- Were proper response procedures in place for the attacks?
- Were the response procedures followed?
  - Was the event escalated properly?
  - Were access control alarms investigated?

The answers to the above questions can be used to evaluate the effectiveness of your current awareness program. Assessment results can also be used to update existing policy and modify detection device configuration for physical and cyber mechanisms. For maximum effectiveness, defenses should be evaluated on a regular basis. Phishing and phone assessments should be performed biannually at minimum. Physical assessments should be performed on an annual basis if your budget allows.

Educate Employees

Describing an attack can be informative, but showing an attack has a far greater impact. The best training session I have ever attended was for a government agency and began with a video of an agency employee telling an adversary sensitive details of a critical defense project. Except the "adversary" was an undercover agent attempting to social engineer information from him; and it worked. Once the video was over, the auditorium was absolutely silent. This short, homemade video was a true eye-opener for the audience. It clearly dictated the message "These threats are real and you could be the next target." The remainder of the session went on to detail how these attacks worked and what to do if you suspected that you were being targeted.

Breaking down attack scenarios is an essential step in social engineering education. Showing the audience how each piece of information obtained and how it was used in the attack builds a true understanding of the process. Next, you'll want to discuss tactics for preventing data leaks and other attacks. A few areas to discuss are the following:

- Metadata—Ensure your audience understands metadata and how it is used against them. Provide tutorials on how to remove metadata from documents before publication. Many of the Microsoft Office programs have this functionality built-in, but not enabled.
- Phishing—It's essential that employees know how to identify and report phishing messages. Demonstrating that links can be disguised and how e-mail addresses can be spoofed is way to drive home the message.
- Social media safety—Educate your audience on social media privacy settings. Walk them through step-by-step on how to restrict Facebook profiles, disable location services, and make the material non-company-specific so employees can share it with their family members.
- Your company e-mail address—Never underestimate the significance of your company e-mail address. It should never be used to subscribe to forums, mailing lists, or other special interest groups. Not only does it expose company technology, but also it can also be used to craft spear phishing attacks posing as a mailing list update.
- Phone attacks—Demonstrate caller ID spoofing to reinforce how easily a phone number can be faked. Discuss what employees should do if they receive a suspicious call. How do they report it?
- Physical attacks—As we discussed earlier in the chapter, sometimes, the easiest way into a target environment is literally through the door. Emphasize the impact of tailgating attacks and the procedures for visitors.

The most important step in preventing social engineering attacks is teaching your workforce that it's ok to ask questions. If someone is attempting to tailgate in the door, it's ok for an employee to ask, "Can you scan your badge please?" It's ok to place a caller on hold while you contact their manager for verification. The objective of every awareness program should be to educate employees on reporting suspicious behavior to the security team, not to become security professionals themselves. For many organizations, this will require a culture change. Management is more likely to approve of this paradigm shift if they understand the threat, so be prepared to educate your management on these types of attacks.

Streamline Existing Technology And Policy

While technology alone cannot prevent social engineering attacks, it can minimize the impact of successful ones. Effective defensive technologies likely exist in your environment but could improve with configuration changes. Rather than reviewing configurations line by line, focus on the big picture with brainstorming sessions, beginning with high-level scenarios that involve key technical members of the cyber security team. This tactic is widely used in the defense industry under the term tabletop exercise and usually involves multiple military branches and civilian agencies. A tabletop exercise is a discussion-based event of scripted scenarios in an informal environment. Usually facilitator-led, these exercises enable security teams to walk through an attack scenario step-by-step to review

- current incident response policy
- Continuity of Operations (COOP) plan
- preventative technologies
- detection capabilities
- methods of minimizing impact once exploitation has occurred

The scenarios are designed to encourage constructive discussion and highlight areas that need to be refined in a nonthreatening environment. Tabletop exercises can have a broad scope and include many areas of review, or a narrow focus to highlight specific areas, such as detection and preventative capabilities of deployed technology. A tabletop exercise is inexpensive to perform and can also serve as on-the-job training for new employees. Don't forget to get input from some of the staff that is actually doing the jobs. As some tasks look good on paper, there may be several other related tasks from other groups that are required and are relied on for full support of their job function.

Planning A Tabletop Exercise

The three phases of a tabletop exercise are design, execution, and after-action. The design phase is critical to exercise success and may take days to weeks to complete depending on the size and complexity of the exercise.

The Design Phase

If your organization has not performed a tabletop exercise, it's best to begin with a narrow focused exercise that includes the cyber security team. For SEDF, the main areas of focus include identifying

- potential detection points for phishing-based attacks throughout the network and host operating system
- methods of minimizing the impact of a successful attack with currently deployed technologies
- response policy for social engineering attacks and incident response

It's recommended that each tabletop exercise have one area of focus. This enables participants to concentrate their efforts more effectively. Once the focus has been determined, the scenarios can be created. A scenario is a sequential, narrative account of a hypothetical incident that provides the catalyst for the exercise and is intended to introduce situations that will inspire responses [1]. Each scenario should contain one topic for discussion and discussion points to focus the group on the desired discussion. A few sample scenarios include the following:

- Phishing attack—A group of attackers is targeting your organization with a phishing e-mail that appears to originate from your human resources department. The e-mail states that the employee must complete a privacy policy acknowledgement in order to receive insurance benefits for the year. The link that is displayed in the e-mail appears to direct the employee to the company website; however, once clicked, the employee is directed to a malicious website, which attempts to capture the information entered into the website.
  - Discussion of detection—What current mechanisms are in place to detect suspicious e-mail and/or suspicious links at the host and network level? Can they be configured to block e-mails that contain disguised links?
  - Discussion of minimizing impact—Once the cyber security team has been notified of the malicious e-mail, is it possible to determine what employees received the e-mail? Can the e-mail be deleted from the recipients' mailbox to prevent additional attacks? Is it possible to block the malicious website (both the URL and IP addresses) using a proxy or other device on the network?
  - Discussion of policy—What actions are taken when an employee reports the suspicious message to the cyber security team? What is the process to block access to the malicious website? What information from this attack can be used to further educate the workforce?
- Malicious document—An infected PDF has been identified on the network. Once the PDF is opened, backdoor software is installed on the machine providing the attacker with access to the machine and the corporate network. Corporate antivirus does not detect the backdoor software or malicious PDF. The origin of the PDF has not been determined and the number of infected machines on the network is unknown.

- Discussion of detection—How can compromised machines be identified? Is it possible to detect the communication of the backdoor software to its command and control address(es)?
- Discussion of minimizing impact—Can a proxy or other network device block the command and control traffic? What options exist for removing the infected PDF and backdoor software? Is it possible to determine if data were removed from the infected machines?
- Discussion of policy—What analysis steps are performed when a suspicious file has been identified? What authorizations are required to modify detection signatures in endpoint and/or proxy policy? What information from this attack can be used to further educate the workforce? Which departments should be notified of the attack?

Tabletop exercises require the following roles:

- Facilitator—The facilitator's role is to create an environment that encourages dialogue and guide discussions to meet the objectives of the exercise [2]. Consider hiring an experienced consultant to facilitate the exercise, as facilitating is a specialized skill. The consultant will have a neutral opinion of the participants, enabling a constructive exercise without favoritism. Lastly, an outsider view of the company network can spark new ideas for discussion.
- Data collector—The data collector's purpose is to document the main discussion points of each scenario and any decisions that were reached during the tabletop exercise. The data collector will also produce the after-action report summarizing the exercise.
- Participants—Select participants whose job responsibilities are related to the exercise focus, not just managers. For detection and minimizing impact exercises, it may be useful to include key employees involved in network and endpoint implementation in addition to the cyber security team. Policy-based exercises should include representatives from each department with a named role in the current policy.

Logistics, equipment, and documentation should also be included in the design phase. Some organizations choose to conduct their exercises off-site at a meeting space or hotel conference room to focus the participants by removing the distractions of their typical day in the office. The exercise location should be a large enough space to comfortably accommodate the number of exercise participants and include an overhead projector, white board, and adequate power resources for participant laptops. Upon arrival, each participant should receive a participant guide. Participant guides should include

- purpose for the exercise
- scope and objectives
- exercise scenarios
- supporting material (network diagrams or policies)

The facilitator guide should include the same material as the participant guide along with the facilitator questions that are to be asked during each scenario. Data collection sheets should include the following columns:

- Problem or objective
- Department affected
- Current response actions or technology
- Resolution or recommendation

The Execution Phase

The exercise should begin with comments from the cyber security management before introducing the facilitator. The facilitator should ask each participant to introduce themselves and their role in the organization. Although most employees are familiar with individual roles and responsibilities, the facilitator is not. The facilitator then provides a high-level overview of the exercise schedule and ground rules. The ground rules are meant to foster a neutral environment for exchange of ideas. A few example ground rules are the following:

- There are no right or wrong answers. All ideas are welcome and will be captured and acted on as appropriate.
- Maintain a no-fault, stress-free environment. It's very important that discussion is driven by group decision-making and problem-solving, so the environment must remain open, positive, and encouraging.
- Use the scenario to provide context and spark creative ideas. All ideas and thoughts should be based on the information provided by the scenario, but this should not limit your thinking.
- Do not limit the discussion to official positions or policies. Don't be afraid to go beyond your title/position as you think about the situations that are presented [2].

The facilitator should introduce the first scenario. If the participants have no questions regarding the scenario events, the facilitator should ask the first question listed for the scenario and then step back and let the participants discuss. If the group begins to focus on topics that are not relevant to the exercise scope, the facilitator will guide the discussion back to the scenario. At the end of each scenario, the group should conduct a hot wash. A hot wash is a high-level overview of the scenario, discussion points, and conclusions. Not only does a hot wash ensure that the participants agree on the conclusions, but also it validates that the data collector has retained the proper information.

It is important to include breaks in the exercise timeline for participants to refuel on caffeine and get fresh air. If the scenarios are too drawn out, attention spans will begin to dwindle, resulting in less discussion. A typical timeline consists of 90 minute sessions with 20 minute breaks in between. Lunch should be served in an outdoor location if possible, to provide participants with a change of environment.

Once participants have completed the last scenario, perform a hot wash of the entire exercise. Some sample questions to ask are the following:

- What are some of the key takeaways from today's exercise?
- Are there suggestions to improve the quality of this exercise regarding
  - venue
  - participants
  - supporting documentation
- What objectives should be included in the next exercise?

The After-action Phase

Information from the data collector is analyzed and compiled to produce a report detailing the exercise events. Next comes the most critical portion of the exercise, creating and assigning action items from the exercise report. Information from the exercise will only be useful to the organization if it is acted upon. Therefore, assigning and tracking action items is crucial to the success of the exercise process. The exercise organizers should conduct a postexercise meeting to discuss the following:

- Was the exercise successful?
- Were appropriate personnel included?
- Was the facilitator sufficient?
- Did the venue provide adequate space and power resources?
- What actions can be taken to improve future exercises?

Many resources exist for exercise planning. The Federal Emergency Management Agency (FEMA) has a complete cyber exercise package available at http://www.fema.gov/media-library/assets/documents/26845.

Preventative Tips

In addition to the outcomes of brainstorming sessions and tabletop exercises, here are some recommendations for hardening your environment against social engineering attacks:

- Username makeover—Attackers can enumerate usernames easily using tactics discussed earlier in the chapter, such as gathering names via social media. Usernames that are not based on names or any other identifiable characteristics complicate social engineering attacks because the attacker isn't able to quickly determine the username associated with the employee they wish to target. Instead of using vthomas for a username, consider a unique identifier such as HN90346283. Not only would this change make actions more difficult for attackers, but also it would make threat detection and log analysis easier for the cyber security team. Login attempts from usernames that stray from the unique identifiers would be an obvious attempted attack, enabling the cyber security team to properly investigate the involved machines. Because this type of change would impact everyone in the organization, the initial stages of deployment may have negative effects, such as an increase of help desk calls from employees that have forgotten their new username. A username makeover would also require support from senior management, as it would require a culture change for the organization to utilize the new format.

- Domain purchases—Social engineers prey on their victim's inability to spot small details in attacks. A popular tactic for phishing attacks is to purchase a domain similar to the target's primary domain. For instance, if your primary domain is www.myorganization.com, an attacker would purchase www.myogranization.com or www.my-organization.com so that the malicious link would appear legitimate at first glance. These malicious domains can also be used to attack your organization's customers if they mistype your website address and inadvertently visit the attacker's website. Creating e-mail accounts from the malicious domain adds credibility to phishing messages, as the e-mail address appears to be from within your organization. Purchasing domains that are similar to your organizations will decrease the risk of attackers using fictitious websites and e-mail addresses to lure their targets. Include popular domain extensions such as .org and .net in your purchases for maximum prevention.
- Webmail addresses—Registering webmail addresses, such as myorganizationadmin@yahoo.com, reduces the likelihood of an attacker utilizing a webmail provider to launch phishing attacks. If an attacker is unable to purchase a convincing domain or create a convincing webmail account, the chances of their attacks being detected by spam filters increases.

Putting It All Together

The SEDF provides a high-level road map for organizations to identify areas that require improvement in order to prevent, detect, or respond to social engineering attacks (Figure 7.1). The phases do not have prerequisites and can be performed in any order you choose.

The key to successfully implementing the framework is to create environment changes based on the results of each phase. Environment changes can include technology, policy, employee education, organizational culture, or modifications to physical security controls. Preventing social engineering attacks is a continuous process, which will require periodic repetitions of each SEDF phase.

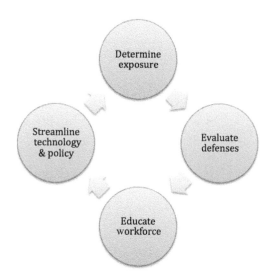

FIGURE 7.1 Phases of the social engineering defensive framework.

WHERE CAN I LEARN MORE ABOUT SOCIAL ENGINEERING?

I've barely scratched the surface of social engineering and how it works in this short chapter. I highly recommend the following books:

- The Art of Deception, The Art of Intrusion, and Ghost In the Wires by Kevin Mitnick
- Catch Me If You Can by Frank W. Abagnale
- No Tech Hacking by Johnny Long

Notes

[1] Tabletop Exercises for Incident Response Plans https://ics-cert.us-cert.gov/sites/default/files/ICSJWG-Archive/F2010/Simon%20-%20Tabletop%20Exercise%20Webinar.pdf [accessed on 5.22.2014].

[2] Cyber Security Tabletop Exercise http://www.fema.gov/media-library-data/20130726-1834-25045-1623/nle_12_ttx___facilitator_s_notes_5.10.12_final__508.pdf.

CHAPTER 8

Physical Security

Valerie Thomas
Securicon, Lorton, VA, USA

WHAT IS PHYSICAL SECURITY?

Physical security describes security measures that are designed to control access to a building, facility, or resource from unauthorized personnel. Unauthorized personnel include attackers who wish to cause harm to the protected environment and accidental intruders, such as employees who may not be aware of the restricted area [1]. Physical security can be divided into three basic levels: outer perimeter security, inner perimeter security, and interior security.

Outer Perimeter Security

The property lines define the outer perimeter. For some organizations, this includes one building; for others, it is a campus of multiple buildings and parking facilities. The goal of securing the outer perimeter is to control who can walk or drive onto the property [2].

Inner Perimeter Security

The inner perimeter consists of outside-facing doors, windows, and walls of your building(s). Controlling who enters and exits the building (and when) is the goal of securing the inner perimeter.

Interior Security

The inside of the building(s) forms the interior security level. The goal of interior security is to only provide appropriate access to portions of the building(s) to authorized employees. This is implemented not only for security but also for employee safety in environments that contain hazardous chemicals or working conditions.

PHYSICAL SECURITY LAYERS

The physical security layers incorporate various methods and tools to support their purpose. Portions of these layers will be included in all three levels of physical security discussed above.

Deterrence

The deterrence layer includes environmental structures that can impede or stop an attack from occurring. Examples of these are as follows:

- Fences
- Gates
- Razor wire
- Speed bumps
- Checkpoints
- Vehicle barriers
- Vehicle height restrictions
- Trenches
- Lighting
- Warning signs

These structures can be combined to funnel the number of entry and exit points of the outer perimeter and create multiple checkpoints.

Control

Physical security control refers to capabilities that limit access to restricted areas. Control features are utilized at all levels of security. Controls can be mechanical, procedural, or electronic. Examples include the following:

- Turnstiles or mantraps
- Electronic card systems
- Mechanical keys
- Combination safes and doors
- Authorization by guard force
- Sign-in book
- Access via security escort

In addition to access control, many of these items provide accountability. Electronic or paper sign-in and sign-out logs can be used as proof of admittance into the controlled building or room.

Detection

Detection and alert systems trigger a response when unauthorized access is detected. The goal of detection devices is to alert physical security personnel of a possible intrusion. Some examples include the following:

- Motion sensors for alarm system or lights
- Alarm functionality of electronic card systems
- Glass break detectors

If your organization employs a guard force, these devices will alert them to the area of concern for further investigation. Some organizations do not have a guard force and rely on police response to alarm systems.

Identification

The identification layer focuses on video monitoring. Although video cameras can be used as a deterrent and detection device, their primary purpose if for historical analysis. If a detection device alerts, a video camera can be used to verify activity in the area. If an attack has already occurred, video footage can be used to identify the attacker and the damage caused by their attack.

THREATS TO PHYSICAL SECURITY

Attackers are not the only threat to physical security. The three main types of physical security threats are as follows:

- External—Often referred to as natural threats. This includes fire, flooding, earthquakes, hurricanes, and tornados.
- Internal—This category includes unintentional acts of destruction such as bad plumbing or wiring, spilled drinks, operator error, and dropped equipment.
- Human—Considered intentional acts of destruction. These threats include theft, vandalism, sabotage, and espionage. Hacking can incorporate one or more of these threats depending on the goals of the attacker [3].

WHY PHYSICAL SECURITY IS IMPORTANT TO AN AWARENESS PROGRAM

Physical security is often managed separately from cyber security; however, both divisions are protecting the same mission: critical items, corporate infrastructure, and intellectual property. While both divisions protect the same

Cyber security	Physical security
Protects valuable assets	Protects valuable assets
Reports to Technology or Financial Officers	Reports to Administration or Facilities Officers
Hires employees with years of specialized experience and education	Hires employees with minimal experience and education
Controls are designed and implemented by network and security professionals	Controls are designed and implemented by eletrical contractors

FIGURE 8.1 The split personality of security.

assets, cyber security is perceived as the more specialized career path. This perception creates a split personality of security, as depicted in Figure 8.1.

An organization can have a multimillion-dollar cyber security program with the latest technology and specialized staff, but if an attacker can simply walk into their building and obtain network access, the security implementation is flawed. As mentioned in Chapter 7, physical security breaches and social engineering go hand in hand. Employee awareness of physical security is crucial to the success of protecting the organization's information and employee safety. In order to properly educate your employees on physical attacks, we've detailed the typical steps that a Red Team, or physical assessment team, would follow to obtain unauthorized access to a building or campus.

HOW PHYSICAL ATTACKS WORK

Organizations often hire security companies to perform a physical penetration assessment. Physical penetration testing evaluates a target facility's controls for prevention of entry, delay of entry, and in some cases response time of security forces. The assessment objectives may vary depending on the organization's largest physical security concerns. Some sample objectives include the following:

- Gaining access to the interior perimeter
- Gaining access to any or all portions of a building
- Obtaining access to the data center or other high-profile target
- Obtaining sensitive information through technical or nontechnical means
- Gaining network and/or computer access

The basic process for physical security assessments has three phases: reconnaissance, attack planning, and attack execution. Similar to social engineering attacks, most of the assessment team's time is spent in the reconnaissance and planning phases.

Reconnaissance

Quality reconnaissance is crucial to the success of a physical attack. Put yourself in the assessment team member's shoes. If you were going to walk into a building unauthorized, wouldn't you want to have as much information as possible before the attack? It is most likely that the assessment team is not physically located within close proximity of the target facility. Most organizations will not fund several weeks of travel for an assessment team to perform reconnaissance, thus creating the need for off-site and on-site reconnaissance.

Off-Site Reconnaissance

A large amount of information can be obtained about an organization utilizing various Internet resources. Gathering as much information as possible on the target's location, physical surroundings, floor plan, day-to-day operations, and security controls in this phase will increase the assessment team's chances of success. The primary areas of off-site reconnaissance are discussed below.

Maps

The first course of action in off-site reconnaissance is getting the lay of the land. Thanks to Google and Bing maps, this is easier than ever (Figure 8.2). Both map programs offer an aerial and, in most cases, street view of locations in the United States.

FIGURE 8.2 Aerial image from Google Maps.

Understanding the target facility and surrounding area is the main focus of the off-site reconnaissance phase. Online maps and street-level images are used to

- identify perimeter security mechanisms including fences, gates, and checkpoints
- locate building parking lots or garages
- identify potential entry points including doors, loading dock, and underground parking
- identify location of dumpsters
- view the surrounding area

The age-old real estate saying "location, location, location" also applies to the physical assessment world. A target's surrounding area plays a large role in the assessment dynamics. One of the most important goals of the off-site reconnaissance phase is to locate potential on-site reconnaissance areas. If the target is located in a heavily populated area surrounded by office buildings, coffee shops, and restaurants, the assessment team will have many on-site reconnaissance areas. However, if the target is located in a rural area, on-site reconnaissance options may be extremely limited. In some heavily populated areas, you may be able to view your target area near real time by utilizing Internet traffic and weather cameras (Figure 8.3). Google Maps provide a web camera option for select locations.

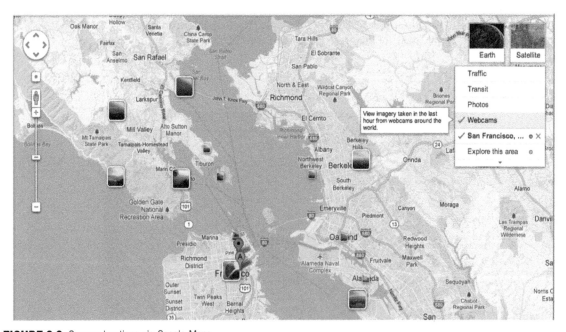

FIGURE 8.3 Camera locations via Google Maps.

In addition to Google Maps, searching for city-sponsored traffic and weather cameras may also provide valuable results.

The Company Website

While information listed on the company website may be considered mundane, it can provide a wealth of information to a physical assessment team. The key pieces of information from the company website include the following:

- Operating hours—Often listed with customer service and public relations phone numbers, the operating hours provide insight as to when the target building may be empty or have minimal employees present. If the company website indicates that 24/7 customer service is available, then call center staff may be on-site throughout the night.
- Address specifics—It is doubtful that the physical assessment team will gain access to a floor plan during this phase. However, by examining mailing address or employee directory details, the team may be able to create a route estimate of a floor map. For example, if the address for customer service is listed as 145 East Main Street, 2nd floor, the assessment team can begin creating a rough building floor plan.
- Information from photos—Photos can be a valuable source of information for the assessment team. Companies often include photos of their building lobby area, fitness center, sundry shop, and other common areas of the building. These photos can be combined to provide the assessment team a basic layout of what is behind the building's front door. Additionally, information can be gathered on the security posture of the organization by locating security cameras, alarm panels, ID card readers, and employee ID cards in the background of company photos.

Additional Sources

The company website and map programs are not the only useful sources of information for attackers. Often, information can be obtained from real estate companies, construction permits, and social media:

- Tax records—Analyze the tax records of the target building to determine if the property is owned by the company or by a real estate company. In addition to ownership, details regarding total square footage and property lines may be obtained from tax records.
- Real estate companies—If the target building is owned by a real estate company, their website may provide detailed information on the building's features including fitness center, underground parking, on-site security monitoring, and rental car service. Real estate companies often have multiple photos of the interior and exterior of the building to attract potential clients. These photos are analyzed for information similar to photos from the company website. Additionally, it may be possible to

determine if the target organization leases the entire building or portions of it. A quick phone call to the real estate agent can confirm building availability. Assessment team members often approach real estate companies as a fictitious business that is interested in leasing space in the target building and schedule a tour of the available office space during their on-site reconnaissance phase.

- Social media—Social media is utilized to provide the assessment team with a list of employees. Searching popular networking websites, such as LinkedIn, can provide team members with names, job titles, and photos of the target company's employees. Additionally, other social media websites are utilized to gather and analyze photos uploaded by employees that may provide ID card photos or other useful information.

Upon completing the off-site reconnaissance phase, the assessment team has an understanding of

- what buildings are in scope of the assessment
- building surroundings
- potential locations to perform on-site reconnaissance
- basic perimeter security knowledge
- the ownership or lease of the building
- operating hours
- basic view of the lobby area
- ID card readers in use
- public events that could provide access to the building
- street-level view of entrances
- potential smoking areas

On-Site Reconnaissance

While the majority of the research occurs during off-site reconnaissance, on-site reconnaissance focuses on observing building operations and employee awareness. The goal of the on-site reconnaissance phase is to have gathered adequate information to plan the attack.

Surveillance

Upon arriving at the target location, team members will drive or walk past the building to observe the level of activity and time of observation. The objective is to determine the level of activity at various times throughout the day and night. Performing the initial drive by at night is preferred, as the building is not likely to be highly occupied. The goals for night surveillance include the following:

- Identify if guard force is present.
- Document if lights are on in specific areas of the building.

- Determine if cleaning crew is present after hours.
- Locate dumpster and assess security controls around it.
- Document if employees enter or exit the building.

If the dumpster appears to be unguarded, the assessment team may perform a dumpster dive to retrieve discarded sensitive information.

Daytime surveillance can be performed in a number of locations throughout the day. Team members will distribute themselves in order to observe all sides of the building. Not all surveillance is performed in a car using binoculars. In highly populated areas, the best surveillance locations are often in public places such as coffee shops, restaurants, benches along the sidewalk, or circling the area on foot. Assessment team members often alter their appearance with clothing, hats, and accessories to avoid suspicion of a single person within close proximity of the building for an extended time. Daytime surveillance objectives include the following:

- Identify smoking areas, as they are ideal locations for gathering information or tailgating into the building.
- Document entry and exit observations for each entrance. Do employees hold the door open for each other?
- Document when the majority of employees report for work in the morning and leave in the evening.
- Determine if parking area is controlled via radio frequency identification (RFID) transponders.
- If the building offers an hourly car rental service through companies such as Zipcar or Hertz, reserve the car and document if an RFID tag is present.
- Obtain photographs of employee ID cards. Most employees wear them in public areas, such as a coffee shop.
- Document if guard staff are present and their locations throughout the facility.
- Document employee attire. If the team members plan to impersonate an employee, they need to dress accordingly.

As you can see, simply observing and documenting the activity around a building can provide an attacker with a plethora of information on its security posture.

Real Estate Meeting

If the assessment team was able to schedule a meeting with the building real estate agent prior to arrival, only one or two team members will attend the meeting to prevent raising suspicion. A guided tour of the building is the ideal opportunity for the team members to observe building operations and ask questions pertaining to the building and office space. If possible, the team will select an available office space on the same floor as the target company and an additional space on a separate floor. Some of the questions the assessment team will ask include the following:

- Does the building require an access card for entry?
- Do individual office spaces require the same access card or separate access card?
- Is 24/7 access available?
- Does the building have on-site guard staff?
- Is office cleaning included in the monthly rent?
- When does the cleaning crew access the office space?
- Do the office spaces have alarm systems?

In addition to the listed questions, the team members should inquire about other details (nonsecurity-related) of the office space to avoid raising suspicion.

RFID Credential Stealing

Many organizations utilize RFID access systems to prevent unauthorized entry into their facilities. These access systems rely on ID cards and card readers to verify a person's access level. Most ID cards are proximity-based. When the ID card is held up to the reader, it receives power from the reader in order to verify its contents. Door controllers and servers then determine if the presented credentials are permitted into the secured area. Reading and reproducing the contents of the ID card can compromise some RFID access card systems. The two popular devices for RFID credential capture are the Proxmark3 and the Bishop Fox Long-range RFID Stealer. These devices can read and store the contents of RFID cards that are within read range. The two main challenges with these devices are getting close enough to the target person without raising suspicion and transporting the necessary power and antenna hardware. Some designs include attaching the hardware to the inside of a binder using Velcro. At first glance, the binder appears unmodified. However, compartments conceal the Proxmark3, power supply, and antenna (Figures 8.4–8.6).

Another mobile design for the Proxmark3 includes securing the components to an organizer with elastic bands (Figure 8.7). The organizers are commercially available in a number of sizes.

The organizer holds the required components and cables in place during movement. Assessment team members then insert the organizer into a basic laptop sleeve to carry without raising suspicion.

Although the Proxmark3 is easy to transport, the range at which it can read ID card contents is approximately 6 in. Positioning the disguised Proxmark3

FIGURE 8.4 Binder to conceal Proxmark3 hardware.

FIGURE 8.5 The Proxmark3 and power supply inside the binder.

within 6 in. of a person's ID card is fairly difficult, even in highly populated areas. To solve this problem, employees at Bishop Fox created a Long-range RFID Stealer [4]. The design utilizes a long-range RFID card reader, as shown in Figure 8.8.

The designers modified the device to include stand-alone power, data storage, and display features (Figure 8.9).

FIGURE 8.6 The antenna inside the binder.

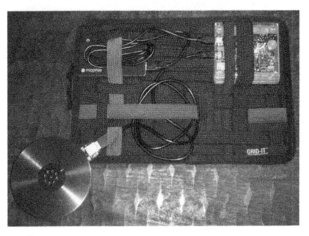

FIGURE 8.7 Proxmark3 with organizer.

The modified card reader first reads the card contents, displays the data on the LCD, and then writes the card contents to a microSD card for analysis on a computer. The assessment team utilizes RFID credential stealing technology during on-site reconnaissance to collect ID card information. Once the card information is collected and analyzed, the team will write the appropriate electronic content to an ID card. Finally, the team members will create a fictitious

FIGURE 8.8 Commercial long-range RFID reader.

FIGURE 8.9 Bishop Fox Long-range RFID Stealer.

ID card printout, including the team member's picture; attach it to the programmed ID card; and laminate the finished product. This process produces an ID card that will most likely pass basic visual inspection and access control systems.

Attack Planning

During the planning phase, the assessment team analyzes the collected data to determine the best course of action to execute the attack. Key decision points for planning the attack include the following:

- When is the ideal time to attack?
  - During business hours
  - After business hours when cleaning crew is present
  - After business hours when the building is empty
- What is the primary approach?
  - Masquerading as an employee
  - Accessing after business hours when a cover identity is not required
  - Claiming to be from a telecommunications provider or vendor
  - Masquerading as a cleaning crew employee
- What is the secondary approach in case the primary approach fails?
- What accessories do the team members need for their assigned duties?
  - Appropriate clothing (cleaning crew uniform or company polo shirt)
  - Tools associated with duties
  - ID cards
  - Business cards
  - Authorization letter from the target company in case of containment

Attack Execution

The attack execution phase is the shortest phase in the physical attack process. It is essential that assessment team members have contact with each other during the attack. If the primary attack fails, the team can execute the secondary attack immediately. Bluetooth headsets and handheld radios are the most popular communication mechanisms for assessment teams. Once the attack has succeeded and the team is inside, typical steps include the following:

- Taking photographs to prove the team's success.
- If the team is also performing a network penetration test, custom malicious backdoors will be uploaded to desktops of employees that have elevated access. These employees were discovered prior to the physical attack using social networking.
- Obtaining access to the server room or data center.
- Collecting sensitive data that are openly displayed on desks, under keyboards, and in file cabinets.
- Obtaining access to senior management offices.

The assessment team is usually on-site for approximately 20 minutes, depending on the security-monitoring schedule. Generally, the assessment team spends as little time as possible on-site to avoid discovery.

MINIMIZING THE RISK OF PHYSICAL ATTACKS

As detailed above, physical attacks require intense and time-consuming research. However, most of the information utilized to plan the attack was publicly available. The most popular method for assessing your organization's risk of physical attack is to perform a physical security assessment, or physical penetration test. Typically performed by specialized consultants, a physical penetration test can highlight areas of potential weakness.

Preparing for a Physical Assessment

If you haven't performed a physical security assessment in the past, there are specific planning steps to be taken to ensure satisfactory results.

Set an Objective

A clear objective is one of the most crucial planning items for a physical security assessment. What areas of your physical security program concern you the most? Common objectives include the following:

- Gaining access to a controlled area, such as the data center
- Bypassing perimeter security controls
- Evaluating electronic security controls

Some organizations elect to perform a zero-knowledge physical security assessment. This type of assessment provides the assessment team with no background information and allows the team to compromise any security control to gain access to as many facilities as possible.

Declare Off-Limits Areas

List specific areas that the assessment team is not authorized to enter. Some organizations work with hazardous material that could harm the assessment team. The company president's office is often declared an off-limits area for physical security assessment.

Schedule

Select a range of acceptable dates and time for the assessment team to perform the attack. Ensure that key personnel, such as the director of physical security and the CIO, are readily available to confirm the assessment team's objective and identify in case the assessment team is discovered.

Authorization Letter

Often referred to as a "get out of jail free card," the authorization letter lists the team members by name along with a summary of their assessment objective.

Employee names, such as the director of physical security, and phone numbers should be listed for guard forces to contact and verify the authorized activity.

A physical security assessment can be an eye-opening experience for even the most sophisticated of organizations. Above all, it is a practical learning experience that will provide valuable insight to improving your organization's physical security posture.

Can't Afford A Physical Security Assessment?

While physical security assessments provide value and insight into currently deployed defense mechanisms, they come at a price. If your organization can't afford a physical security assessment from an outside vendor, there are prevention steps that can be applied without outside assistance:

- Perform your own reconnaissance—Your organization's cyber or physical security team can perform the steps listed in the reconnaissance phase. This nonintrusive evaluation can reveal several vulnerabilities in the physical security program.
- Complete security walk-throughs—A security walk-through is another nonintrusive evaluation that involves reviewing the information that is left exposed on desks or public places. Locating several pieces of sensitive information that has been mishandled could point to a lack of employee awareness.
- Watch the doors—Simply observing how employees enter and exit the building can provide valuable information on the status of physical security awareness. If employees are holding doors open for people behind them, enforcing a strict ID card scanning policy may eliminate tailgating.

Physical security is much more than fences and security guards. Incorporating physical security threats into your awareness program will improve overall security for your organization.

Notes

[1] Physical Security http://www.police.psu.edu/physical-security/what-is-physical-security.cfm [last accessed 25 May 2014].

[2] How to Secure Your Building and Property http://bizsecurity.about.com/od/physicalsecurity/a/What_is_physical_security.htm [last accessed 25 May 2014].

[3] Protecting Your System: Physical Security http://nces.ed.gov/pubs98/safetech/chapter5.asp [last accessed 29 April 2014].

[4] RFID Attack Tools http://www.bishopfox.com/resources/tools/rfid-hacking/attack-tools/ [last accessed 26 May 2014].

CHAPTER 9

Types of Training

Valerie Thomas
Securicon, Lorton, VA, USA

TRAINING TYPES

Several options exist for presenting your training material. In this chapter, we'll discuss various training techniques and their pros and cons. This chapter presents a high-level overview of training techniques. In chapters to come, we'll discuss how to package or blend these techniques to suit your environment.

FORMAL TRAINING

We'll begin with types of formal training. Formal training is a controlled and structured approach, which typically involves material based on written regulations or standards, policies, or a set of requirements [1]. The content development process is usually labor-intensive, as most programs require development of courseware. Evaluations, such as quizzes, are usually completed after content delivery to assess the employee's understanding and retention of the presented material.

In-Person Training

In-person training, or instructor-led training, is considered a traditional approach in training techniques. Typically, this includes the use of slideshows that are custom-built for the target audience. However, it does not need to be limited to slideshows alone. Other delivery methods can be used to convey material including the following:

- Video: Including short video segments breaks the monotony of a lecture by providing the audience with a visual focus point. This method is best for demonstrating a threat, such as tailgating.
- Storytelling: Storytelling is a great way to put a personal spin on a lecture. It enables the instructor to provide examples of situations

where employees followed procedure or sought guidance from their security division. Storytelling also enables the instructor to provide an example of material covered previously in the course to reaffirm the message [2].

While the main delivery method of the session is lecture from the instructor, other methods can be used to incorporate audience interaction. The discussion method usually begins with a short lecture including basic information and is followed by open discussion or questions (from the instructor or the audience) to provide clarification on the material. Asking the audience to identify indicators of a phishing e-mail is an example of the discussion method [3].

Advantages
- Instructor-led training is effective for presenting a large amount of material to a large group of people.
- Sessions can be recorded and replayed at a later time, for example, new employee orientation. These recordings can also be used for remote offices.
- Slideshows can be archived on the security department's website for on-demand viewing.
- The instructor can address questions from the audience immediately.
- There is an opportunity for follow-up discussion with the instructor and other members of the audience.
- If led by a member of the security department, it provides a person for employees to associate to the security department. If presented properly, this can depict a two-way communication path that encourages employees to interact with the security department, as opposed to dictating rules.

Disadvantages
- The success of the session is highly dependent on the skill level of the instructor.
- Audience members may not have the opportunity to ask questions if the assigned time window is too short or if the session is being played from a recording.
- Scheduling a classroom sessions for large groups is often difficult in terms of available space and employee schedules.
- It can be difficult for employees who speak English as a second language to retain material at the speed of the instructor.
- Hiring an instructor can be costly, especially if they are visiting multiple locations

- Employees may become overwhelmed from attempting to retain a large amount of data presented in a short amount of time
- It can be difficult for employees to search through an entire training session to locate one specific topic [4].

Computer-Based Training

The use of computer-based training (CBT) has grown rapidly over the years, in some cases replacing in-person training altogether. CBT is delivered through a computer and can utilize a magnitude of delivery options such as text, audio, video, interactive quizzes, and many more. However, CBT material is stored locally on a hard drive or distributed via CD-ROM. Material is often created solely for the organization to fit their requirements at a certain point in time [3].

Advantages
- On-demand viewing. Employees can review material at a time that's convenient for them.
- Material can be completely customized for the organization.
- It can be produced in-house but is commonly outsourced.
- Distributing via CD-ROM is ideal for remote locations with limited bandwidth, such as a military base.
- Courses are self-paced so employees can learn at a speed that's best for them.

Disadvantages
- These distribution options can be difficult to modify or update to reflect current security threats or policy changes.
- Content modification can be expensive if an outside company produced the material.
- Content medication can be complicated if the material was developed in-house by an employee who is no longer with the organization.
- Redistribution can be logistically difficult, especially for remote locations.
- If the material is poorly designed, employees may lose interest quickly and not retain any of the presented material.

Web-Based Training

Web-based training (WBT) is similar to CBT but is housed online via a company web server or by an external training provider. Because the content is stored in a small number of locations, it is easy to update. Courses can be integrated into a training portal that enables the organization to offer multiple courses and electronically track each employee's progress. This delivery vehicle makes it easy to create targeted training for different audiences such as the help desk or marketing. WBT is a great method for delivering material small, focused sessions, such as phishing awareness. Many of the advantages are similar to CBT in addition to others.

A NOTE ABOUT QUIZZES

Quizzes are fantastic for measuring the employee's learning progress in web-based training. However, if the employee answers a question incorrectly, it is crucial to provide a follow-up page to explain why the answer was incorrect.

WBT has the flexibility to feature video segments from industry professionals in addition to slideshow material. The combination of delivery methods divides the material into segments, making it easier to comprehend. Employees can also replay video segments if they were not able to keep up with the pace of the speaker.

Interactive segments and quizzes can assess the knowledge retained from the presented material with the option of follow-on training based on the employee's answer. Some commercial product vendors are Symantec, KnowBe4, and SANS.

Advantages
- Access to highly specialized trainers and course developers at a lower cost than hiring for a one-time in-person session. [5].
- On-demand viewing. Employees can review material at a time that's convenient for them.
- Ideal for specialized training, such as regulatory requirements.
- Material can be completely customized for the organization.
- Content can be integrated into a training portal, which enables progress tracking for each employee.
- It can be produced in-house but is commonly outsourced.
- Content can be easily updated.
- A combination of slideshow, video, and interactive content can effectively communicate material.

Disadvantages
- Employees may have questions that are not addressed by the frequently asked questions (FAQ).
- If the training session is too long or uninteresting, employees will likely click through the content without retaining the material.

- Browser and/or bandwidth limitations may restrict the ability to use video or interactive sessions [6].
- If outsourced, initial development cost can be high [7].

Video Training

Video training is viewed stand-alone from other forms of training requiring no interaction from the employee. These segments cover one or two topics in a short amount of time, such as the use of removable media. Video training is most effective when incorporated into a video campaign. A video campaign consists of a set of videos and other supporting materials such as posters, preview videos, announcement e-mails, and a reference sheet to accompany each video.

Advantages
- Puts a new spin on security content, which peaks the interest of employees.
- Allows the employee to focus on learning as opposed to stressing over a quiz on the covered material.
- Commercially produced material is available for immediate use.

Disadvantages
- Readily available commercial products cover general security topics. Customized segments would come at an additional cost.
- Some employees may not find the video entertaining, and therefore not watch the complete segment

INFORMAL TRAINING

Informal training is designed with an overall objective, but without the standards and procedures of formal training. While formal learning is usually required of employees, informal learning is voluntary. Essentially, informal learning provides the means for education, but the employee must decide to pursue the material. While informal learning environments are ideal for some employees, they are not meant to replace formal training programs. Informal learning acts as an additional layer of support to a formal training program [8].

Lunch and Learn Sessions

Usually, short (about 30 min or less) and voluntary sessions lunch and learn presentations or discussions can cover a variety of topics. The key to successful voluntary sessions is selecting topics and titles that will appeal to employees. A few examples are

- keeping your children safe online
- mobile safety tips and tricks
- tap and pay credit cards: what you need to know
- online safety while traveling

Anyone can lead a lunch and learn session. Ideally, members of the security team should rotate sessions so that employees are familiar with all team members. This helps to place a face to the security team and reinforces a two-way dialog. If the budget allows, inviting guest speakers is a great way to increase attendance.

Not all informal sessions need to be intended for a general audience. Consider coordinating with department heads to create lunch and learn sessions that appeal to technical employees as well. Some example topics include

- the top 5 coding mistakes you're making (and how to fix them)
- why developers are a social engineer's favorite target
- whether your LinkedIn profile is saying too much
- advanced routing techniques

Although none of the above titles directly address security, it is possible to include it in the overall message. We'll discuss how to effectively package security training in future chapters.

Homemade Video Campaign

Online video websites such as http://YouTube.com have dramatically changed the way that the world views video content. Short, homemade videos are the new norm in today's society. From dancing cats and giggling babies to software installation procedures and cooking instructions are available to anyone with just a few clicks of a mouse. Like most topics, security awareness training can also use this video craze to its advantage.

Producing short, informal videos for the organization's internal website can reinforce material that has been previously covered in formal training. This virtually no-cost technique can also incorporate the workforce into the education process by featuring the Chief Information Security Office (CISO) forgetting sensitive documents at the printer. Other employees can be featured following procedure, such as challenging someone who is attempting to tailgate into the building.

Things to consider when developing your own video campaign:

- Keep the videos short and entertaining. Less than two minutes is best for retaining the viewer's attention.

- Be sure to reinforce the intended message at the end. If the video featured an employee reporting a suspicious e-mail to the security team, then include the e-mail address for reporting these e-mails.
- Include a short preview of the next video.
- Create an e-mail account for employees to submit ideas for future videos.

Posters

Security awareness posters are a low-cost method to reinforce good security practice principles between formal sessions. The two most important factors of a successful poster campaign are content and placement. Content should have very few words and deliver a clear message. Prime examples of security awareness posters come from the "loose lips sink ships" campaign during World War II. Designed by the War Advertising Council, the campaign was a reminder to all Americans to be discrete with the information they shared to prevent unintentional data leaks to the enemy [9].

Placing the posters in the correct area is the second step to success. Ideally, posters should be placed in areas where employees have idle time. A few examples are as follows:

- In elevators. If the building has more than one elevator, place a unique poster in each elevator car.
- By the copy machine. This is an ideal spot for reminders about securing sensitive data.
- The break room or cafeteria, especially by the microwave.
- Close to the exit door. This can be a final reminder for employees to put their ID cards away and out of plain sight.

Several websites offer free awareness posters for use within your organization. A quick search on the Internet can provide enough free material to support your campaign for months.

Notes

[1] 8 Benefits of Formal and Informal Learning. http://www.langevin.com/blog/2012/05/10/8-benefits-of-formal-and-informal-learning/ [accessed on 2.12.2013].

[2] The Most Effective Training Techniques http://trainingtoday.blr.com/employee-training-resources/How-to-Choose-the-Most-Effective-Training-Techniques [accessed on 8.01.2014].

[3] Training Delivery Methods http://www.referenceforbusiness.com/management/Tr-Z/Training-Delivery-Methods.html [accessed on 12.01.2014].

[4] In-Person Versus Online Training Advantages and Cost Comparison Table. http://www.elearncampus.com/online_training/comparisontable.aspx [accessed on 12.01.2014].

[5] 7 Reasons Why Organizations Use Online Training http://www.knowbe4.com/resources/7-reasons-why-organizations-use-online-training/ [accessed on 27.01.2014].

[6] Web Based Training Advantages and Disadvantages http://www.webbasedtraining.com/primer_advdis.aspx [accessed on 27.01.2014].

[7] Web-based Training Overview http://www.etc.edu.cn/eet/articles/webbtraining/start.htm [accessed on 30.01.2014].

[8] Formal Training Vs. Informal Training: Which Makes More Sense? http://www.mindflash.com/blog/2012/03/formal-training-vs-informal-learning-which-makes-more-sense/ [accessed on 31.01.2014].

[9] Security of War Information - Loose Lips Sink Ships (1942–1945) http://www.aef.com/exhibits/social_responsibility/ad_council/2175 [accessed on 3.02.2014].

CHAPTER 10

The Training Cycle

Valerie Thomas
Securicon, Lorton, VA, USA

THE TRAINING CYCLE

In order for employees to retain knowledge, they'll need to be trained more than once. True education is not a one-shot process. A training cycle should consist of short- and long-term training instances. In this chapter, we'll discuss various options for creating your own training cycle. While reviewing the options, keep in mind that you don't need to implement all of them, just what makes sense for your organization.

NEW HIRE

We've all heard the phrase "You never get a second chance at a first impression." This also applies to awareness training. New hire training is an employee's first glimpse into the inner workings of the organization. If security training is disorganized or incomplete, it can convey that security isn't a priority for the organization or its employees. At a minimum training should

- describe the purpose for security training
- highlight key areas of security policy
- detail the largest threats to the organization
- highlight physical security threats
- teach users how to identify and report suspicious e-mails or activities

New hires should leave this training with an understanding of the listed items above and copies (or locations) of the covered information and security policies for future reference. Additionally, training should be completed prior to granting access to organizational assets.

QUARTERLY

Every employee needs a refresher course; this is occasionally referred to as people patching [1]. Keeping your computer's security up-to-date requires constant vigilance; people require the same level of maintenance or people patching. Although new hire training is essential, in order for employees to retain the concepts long-term, they require periodic refreshers.

Why Quarterly?

Many industry standards require quarterly security awareness training. If your organization is required to comply with these regulations, use it to your advantage. Quarterly training is a fantastic opportunity to update employees on the latest threats and trends. Was the organization targeted with a phishing e-mail? If so, include the message in the training and highlight the suspicious portions. Don't forget to include the procedure for reporting suspicious e-mails.

This is also an ideal vehicle to announce policy changes with details on what has been added or removed. Including an article or two about current attacks will provide real-world application of the covered material.

BIANNUAL

If your management does not support quarterly training, biannual training should be considered the minimum required time frame. Expecting employees to remember something after being taught one time will leave your employees unprepared and frustrated. If training can only occur twice a year, ensure that the content is focused on critical topics to your organization's security. While every organization's priorities are different, a few examples are

- laptop safety and how to report a lost/stolen laptop
- identifying phishing attempts and how to report them
- proper handling of sensitive information
- preventing tailgating

You'll notice that this information appears to be similar to new hire training. The purpose of biannual training is to reinforce the fundamentals described in new hire training without detailing each policy.

CONTINUAL

In Chapter 9, we discussed several variations of informal training. These low-cost programs can reinforce concepts taught in other required training events throughout the year. Implementing continual training keeps security on the minds of employees. A few examples are

- posters with a company laptop forgotten in a public place and the phone number to report security incidents
- e-mail newsletters with on-line safety tips for home use
- implementing log-on banners for employee workstations with a security tip of the day [2]
- lunch and learn sessions about social media safety

POINT OF FAILURE

Point of failure, also known as embedded training, refers to training administered when an employee fails a simulated phishing attack. There are mixed opinions of the effectiveness of point-of-failure training in the industry. Some industry members claim this method of training is ineffective [3] because employees aren't retaining the information presented. Other industry members claim this method of training is extremely effective [4] if implemented properly. If your management does not support quarterly training for everyone, point-of-failure training can educate employees that need it the most.

The key to properly implementing point-of-failure training is frequency of testing. Employees who failed a simulated attack should be tested again within weeks of the failure. This process reinforces the presented material by requiring them to apply learned concepts. However, the simulated phishing attack should not look identical to the failed attack. In Chapter 11, we'll discuss creating your own simulated phishing attacks.

TARGETED TRAINING

Training by department should be included in the annual training cycle. For maximum effectiveness, present this training separately from the general employee training. Presenting the material separately enables the employees to absorb and retain the information long term. Ideally, this targeted training should be conducted quarterly and should focus on no more than three key messages or threats that are unique to each department. Highlight the unique threats facing each organization. Accounts receivable and marketing are at a high risk for macro viruses and malicious PDF documents, because opening documents received from outside the organization is a common activity. The help desk is a prime target for attackers to gain information about computer accounts, corporate policies, operating system details, and organizational structure via fake phone calls to the help desk. Create a list of top threats for each department, and then create training segments that address no more than three specific threats.

SAMPLE TRAINING CYCLES

If your awareness program is new and there is no current cycle in place, it is best to plan a robust training cycle. Gaining approval from management to implement a new training cycle may be easier than gaining approval to modify an existing one. New hire training isn't repeated, so it is not included in the examples below.

Minimal

This cycle is designed to include the recommended minimum training intervals. Integrating the targeted biannually is even more crucial with a minimal training cycle, as it reinforces best practices for those in public-facing positions more than twice per year:

- Biannual training sessions for all employees
- Continual training in the form of newsletters and posters
- Targeted training biannually for public-facing departments

Moderate

Designed for organizations that are able to address more than a minimal training cycle, this cycle incorporates additional elements:

- Biannual training sessions for all employees
- Continual training in the form of video campaigns, lunch and learns, newsletters, and posters
- Targeted training biannually for public-facing departments
- Biannual point-of-failure training for all employees

Robust

This training cycle incorporates multiple elements to expose employees to training roughly every sixty days:

- Quarterly training sessions for all employees
- Continual training in the form of video campaigns, lunch and learns, contests, newsletters, and posters
- Targeted training biannually for public-facing departments
- Quarterly point-of-failure training for all employees

ADJUSTING YOUR TRAINING CYCLE

If you have an existing training cycle in place and metrics indicate that training isn't meeting the targeted goal, it is likely the training cycle requires adjusting. Increasing continual training is a low-cost option. Combining new continual training with additional training type will yield a higher return on investment. Use the metrics to determine which areas of awareness are below average and adjust the training cycle to increase training in those areas. For instance, if phishing detection results were low, consider implementing point-of-failure training to provide instant training for employees who did not pass the phishing assessment. Program metrics are discussed at length in Chapter 13.

Notes

[1] People Patching: Is user education of any use at all? http://www.eset.com/us/resources/white-papers/People_Patching.pdf [accessed on 2.16.2014].

[2] Developing continual healthcare data security training http://healthitsecurity.com/2013/08/05/developing-continual-healthcare-data-security-training/ [accessed on 2.16.2014].

[3] Why Training Doesn't Mitigate Phishing http://www.govinfosecurity.com/interviews/training-doesnt-mitigate-phishing-i-2148? [accessed on 2.17.2014].

[4] SHOCKER: Point-Of-Failure Phishing Training Does Not Work http://blog.knowbe4.com/bid/371048/SHOCKER-Point-Of-Failure-Phishing-Training-Does-Not-Work [accessed on 2.17.2014].

CHAPTER 11

Creating Simulated Phishing Attacks

Valerie Thomas
Securicon, Lorton, VA, USA

SIMULATED PHISHING ATTACKS

Simulated phishing attacks are gaining popularity within organizations for many reasons. When implemented properly, simulated phishing attacks can be utilized as training tools, test resistance to attacks, and provide metrics to management. While simulated phishing attacks are useful, they can also be a bit intimidating if you haven't created one before. In this chapter we'll go through the process step by step and discuss some tools to help along the way. Beginning a simulated phishing campaign can be overwhelming at first. Keep in mind that you aren't testing everyone in your organization at once. These campaigns, or assessments, can easily be divided into small groups.

UNDERSTANDING THE HUMAN ELEMENT

Phishing e-mails prey on a variety of human emotions in order to achieve the desired action [1]. Often, phishing e-mails create a sense of urgency, claiming that the recipient's account will be disabled if immediate action isn't taken. Another popular attack is the e-card e-mail. This attack indicates that someone has sent the user an e-card and they must click on the link to retrieve it. Other tactics to persuade an employee to fall prey to an attack include using their first name or sending an e-mail that appears to be from a fellow employee.

METHODOLOGY

If you wish to incorporate a simulated phishing exercise into your awareness program, here is a high-level methodology [2]:

- Establish a baseline by testing all employees
- Train all employees (using your technique of choice)

- Continue to test employees
- Educate employees with embedded or continual training
- Report results to management
- Make adjustments as necessary

This cycle of events may take weeks if you have a small organization or months if your organization has hundreds to thousands of employees.

OPEN-SOURCE TOOL, COMMERCIAL TOOL, OR VENDOR PERFORMED?

There are many factors to consider when selecting an assessment tool, including

- cost
- number of employees
- built-in training options
- frequency of use
- technical requirements
- ease of use
- long-term metric reporting

Although all of these factors are important, the number of employees in your organization and allotted budget are normally the largest deciding factors.

Open-Source Tool

Open-sourced software/tools is "software with its source code made available and licensed with a license in which the copyright holder provides the rights to study, change and distribute the software to anyone and for any purpose." In short, it's pretty much free. With this, there is most often no guarantee of the software and the effects it will have on your environment. Additionally, support is often limited to software/developer/user forums and limited e-mail responses. While this may seem scary reading the text alone, the majority of penetration testers, vulnerability analysts, and other technical staff in the cyber community use one or several open-source tools to get their job done. Of all the capabilities that these technical staff need, most of them are not made by for-profit companies, hence the reason to rely on the open-source community.

The most popular open-source tool for phishing campaigns is the Social-Engineer Toolkit (SET) by Dave Kennedy of TrustedSec. It is considered the *"de facto"* tool for social engineering (Figure 11.1). SET can be installed on a machine inside or outside of your network, depending on your social engineering scenario.

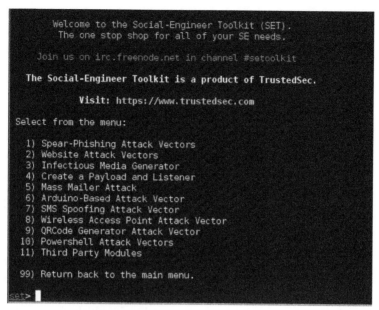

FIGURE 11.1 Main menu of the Social-Engineer Toolkit.

Pros
  Aside from being free, SET offers a variety of resources for phishing campaigns including
  - the ability to clone an existing website for your landing page (page your employees will see/go to from the phishing message)
  - capturing passwords and other information entered on the landing page
  - prompting the user to run a program from the landing page
  - configuring to utilize your organization's e-mail server for ease of delivery
  - the ability to create attachments to include in e-mails
  - integrating with the Metasploit Framework for advanced testing options

Updates are released regularly and documentation is widely available to help you get started. Overall, SET is an incredibly flexible tool for developing custom phishing campaigns for the tech-savvy user.

Cons
  Although SET is a powerful tool, it may not be suitable for all environments for a few reasons:
  - Must be installed on a Linux machine
  - Command-line-based

- Requires basic knowledge of Apache web server and Metasploit Framework
- No long-term metrics are stored in the tool itself. They must be documented from the report and saved elsewhere
- E-mail groups are not stored in the tool and must be maintained separately
- There is no dedicated support center for assistance

SET provides the user with many basic and advanced options for phishing campaigns. Users who are not familiar with Linux, Apache, and Metasploit Framework may find the tool difficult to use. Long-term users will need to track metrics, e-mail groups, and campaign history separately. More information on SET can be found at TrustedSec's website http://www.trustedsec.com.

Commercial Tool

If you prefer a more graphic-based tool, commercial products may be best for you. These products are mainly web-based and hosted through the vendor's infrastructure. In other words, you don't need any hardware or Linux knowledge to get started. The market for phishing campaign tools is rapidly expanding. A few of the most popular vendors are KnowBe4, PhishingBox, and PhishMe.

Pros
- Preconfigured e-mail and landing page templates.
- Ability to change the landing page appearance with a graphic tool instead of modifying the page source code.
- Most products contain built-in training for employees who did not pass the assessment.
- Products are web-based so there's no software to install.
- Many products allow you to utilize your organization's mail server.
- User guides and other documentation are available.
- Support is available from the vendor for questions.

Cons
- Subscription fees
- Some products require a long-term contract
- A minimum number of e-mails per year are usually required

Commercial tools also make it easy to manage multiple assessments at once. Figure 11.2 is the dashboard of PhishingBox. The dashboard highlights assessments that are in progress, scheduled, or awaiting authorization. Selecting an assessment in progress will provide you with up-to-date information of how many e-mails have been opened and more.

FIGURE 11.2 Dashboard Screen of PhishingBox.

The biggest hurdle to getting started with a vendor tool is the import of target e-mail addresses. Most tools require a specific format for e-mail address, name, and department. If you elect to use the vendor's e-mail servers to perform the test, some additional coordination with your e-mail team may be required in order to white list the vendor's servers for ensured mail delivery.

Selecting a Commercial Tool

In order to select the tool best suited for your organization, you should have answers (or estimates) to the following:

- What is you annual budget?
- How many e-mails do you want to send and how often?
- Do you wish to include instant training material for the employees who fail the assessment?
- Do you want to include attachments in your e-mails?

Many vendors offer free trial license and a live demo. Consider making time for the live demo. Not only does it provide you with an overview of the tool, but also it's your opportunity for questions about specific features and functionality. Evaluate a few different tools before making your selection. Some evaluation criteria to keep in mind are

- ease of campaign creation
- quality and quantity of e-mail and landing page templates
- ease of modifying templates
- ability to automatically insert first name and department into an e-mail
- ease of creating your own e-mail and landing page
- report generation and export options
- long-term metric tracking
- e-mail group management
- ability to schedule e-mail delivery
- available user guides and documentation

Vendor Performed

Building a phishing campaign isn't for everyone. If your budget supports a more expensive solution, hiring a vendor to perform the assessment may be for you. Almost all vendors that advertise a phishing campaign tool provide phishing assessments as a professional service. Organizations that only perform phishing assessments once or twice a year usually elect this method.

Pros
- Easy to implement.
- Requires no software purchase or subscription.
- Many vendors do not require a long-term contract.

Cons
- Most expensive solution.
- Long-term metric tracking may not be available.
- Dependent of vendor availability.

Although the vendor will be doing the heavy lifting on most aspects of the assessment, there are items that you as the client must provide including a list of target e-mail addresses and schedule for e-mail delivery. Most importantly, your organization must coordinate internally to prepare for the assessment to avoid confusion among the security team and other key positions in the organization.

BEFORE YOU BEGIN

Operational coordination is essential in this process. Key people in the organization must be informed prior to performing your phishing exercise in order to prevent mistaking a phishing exercise for a real attack. Your Chief Information Security Officer (CISO) must be aware of all planned and active exercises. The manager/handler of the company's incident response team (IRT) should be informed of all exercises prior to execution. The manager may choose to inform their team in order to prevent spending time and resources investing an exercise. The manager may also choose to not inform their team in order to evaluate their response to the attack(s).

Reporting of hacks/penetrations to a company's network is a very sensitive thing. Most do not want to admit that a breach has occurred and try to keep it quiet. While this may "save face" to the company, it does not help all companies overall, as the attack data/vectors could be passed on to prevent breaches elsewhere in the industry. Final authority, unless otherwise explicitly required by law, regulation, or policy, is usually give by the company's CEO and/or board members, in collaboration with the company's legal team and public relations office. If an incident is to be reported to outside agencies, ensure that senior management is involved and that applicable laws/policies are followed.

Informing the manager of the help desk is also a good practice, as they will likely receive calls from targeted employees. While it is uncommon for the help desk manager to inform employees of a potential exercise, they can ensure that procedures for handling suspicious e-mails are up-to-date for their employees to reference. It is also important for the help desk manager to report the number of calls and e-mails received during the exercise.

Create a contact list with information for the included parties. Ensure that each main point of contact also has an alternate contact. Notifications may vary depending on the type of phishing e-mails you select. For instance, if you create an e-mail that appears to originate from human resources, then the human resources manager should be notified prior the phishing exercise. This management level notification prevents confusion and panic if employees begin contacting the originating department.

DETERMINE ATTACK OBJECTIVE

Simulated attacks can be as simple or complex as you'd like. They can be designed to measure many results, including

- click only,
- click and enter information on a landing page,
- click and enter password on a landing page,
- open an attachment.

If your organization hasn't conducted a simulated attack, the click only objective is a good starting point.

SELECT RECIPIENTS

Choosing the employees to evaluate first will help determine the type of attack you want to perform. Employees can be divided into groups for ease of administration. If your organization spans over multiple time zones, be sure to group employees in similar time zones. E-mails received during nonworking hours can be deemed suspicious. For nontechnical employees, general or company-specific types of attacks are most likely to result in clicks. For more technical employees, spear phishing attacks are more likely to result in clicks.

SELECT A TYPE OF PHISHING ATTACK

As discussed earlier, phishing e-mails utilize human emotions deceive their victims. This basically means that the sky is the limit when it comes to selecting e-mail themes.

General

General phishing attacks can be used to target anyone in the organization. These types of e-mails are a good starting point for your first few e-mails. A few themes are as follows:

- Your package has shipped! Click here to track delivery progress.
- Any type of charity seeking donation.
- Someone has sent you an e-card! Click here to retrieve it.

Many of these examples can be utilized throughout the year but are ideal for holidays where cards are used, such as Valentine's Day and the months of November through December. Many purchased solutions have built-in general messages to get you started.

Company-Specific

Ethical hackers when performing a penetration test of the organization's network commonly use these types of attacks. The reasons are simple, the attacks are easy to construct and work the majority of the time. Not only do they work in penetration tests, but also they work in real-life scenarios. With minimal search time, an attacker can locate websites or affiliated partners of the company, such as

- timekeeping software vendor or website,
- web-based e-mail website,
- web-based VPN website,
- health benefits provider.

The information from these websites can be used to mimic legitimate e-mails. Additionally, the websites themselves can be duplicated to lure the employee into entering information, such as their username and password, after clicking the link in the phishing message.

Spear Phishing

According to the software company Trend Micro, 91% of cyber attacks began with a spear phishing e-mail [3]. Spear phishing e-mails target a single person or a small group within an organization. Attackers search a number of sources to deduce an employee's job function and what companies, individuals, or groups they associate with in order to create a believable attack. A spear phishing message

- addresses the recipient by name,
- appears to be sent by a person or vendor that the recipient is familiar with,
- includes a proper signature block with logo and contact information,
- often includes an infected attachment,
- can contain a link to a website similar to the sender's (abcbank.com instead of abc-bank.com)

While other phishing e-mails are sent in large quantities, spear phishing e-mails are sent to very few employees—usually less than five. However, the extra research time usually pays off, as spear phishing messages have the highest rate of success.

COMPOSING THE E-MAIL

Once you've selected your target group and e-mail type, it's time to move on to creating the e-mail content. Here are some of the key elements for creating a realistic phishing message:

- Use an attention-grabbing subject.
- Create a sense of urgency in the message body that will motivate the recipient to take action.
- Include logos and other applicable images.
- Ensure the sender's name and e-mail address match the theme of your e-mail.
- If your e-mail appears to originate from a person, include a complete signature block.
- For e-mails that appear to be automatically generated, include a privacy statement at the end of the e-mail.

If you're using a vendor tool, you can edit the e-mail appearance in a graphic editor. Figure 11.3 is a screenshot of the composition tool by the vendor

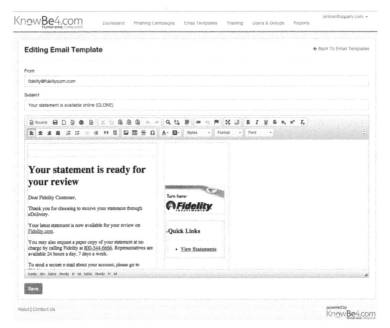

FIGURE 11.3 E-mail composition screen of KnowBe4.

KnowBe4. This particular template includes a landing page (where the browser will go once the link has been clicked), which is displayed to the right. If you're using SET, the e-mail contents need to be plain text with appropriate HTML tags for formatting.

Formatting the Link

Unless you are performing an attack with an attachment, your e-mail will include a link for the employee to click. The appearance of the link, or uniform resource locator (URL), plays an important role in the assessment. If the URL looks suspicious or misspelled, employees are less likely to click.

Graphic editing tools allow you to easily modify the display text of a URL so it appears as http://abc.com but once clicked goes to http://cba.com. Using this technique will educate your employees on URL modification and how to verify a link's true destination before clicking.

CREATING THE LANDING PAGE

The landing page is where the employee will be directed if they click the enclosed link (Figure 11.4). If your assessment objective is to document the number of employees that clicked, this is a prime opportunity to display a

FIGURE 11.4 Basic landing page of KnowBe4.

message informing the employee of the simulated phishing assessment and to present training material.

If the attack objective is to determine if employees will click and enter information, the landing page must have areas that accept input. The most common input is an account password; however, you can customize the landing page to fit the attack objective. All commercial tools have a selection of landing pages that accept input. If you would like to use a webpage that belongs to your organization, most tools have an import feature. SET will clone a website once you have provided the URL.

SENDING THE E-MAIL

Now that you've created the list of recipients, the e-mail, and landing page, there are a few more quality control steps to take before pressing the send button:

- Test appearance of e-mail in your e-mail client and web client (if applicable) by e-mailing the phishing e-mail to yourself.
- Click the enclosed link to test the landing page. If your organization uses multiple browsers then test in all approved browsers.
- Notify involved parties on the contact list as discussed earlier in the chapter. Include screenshots of the e-mail, landing page, and training page (if applicable). Also include the dates and times the e-mails will be sent.

Timing is Everything

When the e-mails are sent, they will significantly impact the results of your assessment. Ideally, the e-mails should be sent when employees are likely to be at their desks midmorning or midafternoon. Also, keep in mind what time zone your recipients are in when scheduling e-mail delivery.

Everyone needs a vacation now and again. If anyone on the contact list will be on vacation during the assessment, be sure to involve their backup contact person prior to sending any e-mails. Additionally, the personnel responsible for sending the e-mails and tracking their progress need to be available for questions. Don't start an exercise and be out of the office the next day.

TRACKING RESULTS

All tools, commercial and open source, have tracking ability to help you monitor the status of your assessment. Although individual tracking features may vary, most tools will indicate

- if the e-mail was opened,
- if recipients clicked the link,
- if information was entered into the landing page,
- if the link was clicked more than once.

Commercial tools will store the result information for each assessment for comparison reporting after additional assessments. SET does not store result information, so record will need to be tracked separately, most likely in a spreadsheet. Comparison reporting is key when reporting results to management and other involved parties to indicate the effectiveness of follow-on training.

Results tracking includes more than number of clicks. Other important results to track include

- help desk calls reporting the e-mail,
- e-mails received reporting the e-mail to security,
- phone calls to security,
- phone calls to involved departments, such as human resources

Improper reporting indicates that employees are not familiar with the procedure to follow after they've received a suspicious message. Training procedures can be adjusted to reinforce the proper procedure.

POST ASSESSMENT FOLLOW-UP

Once the assessment is complete and all results have been documented, take the time for an after action meeting with those individuals on the contact list. Discuss the results of the assessment and if there were any unexpected outcomes. Use this information to make changes to the procedure and contact list for future assessments.

Notes

[1] Open Source Software definition http://en.wikipedia.org/wiki/Open-source_software [accessed on 5.26.2014].

[2] The Seven Habits of Highly Effective Employee Phishing Training http://threatsim.com/resources/whitepaper-seven-habits-phishing [accessed on 2.12.2014].

[3] SHOCKER: Point-Of-Failure Phishing Training Does Not Work http://blog.knowbe4.com/bid/371048/SHOCKER-Point-Of-Failure-Phishing-Training-Does-Not-Work [accessed on 2.17.2014].

[4] 91% of cyber attacks begin with a spear phishing email http://news.techworld.com/security/3413574/91-of-cyberattacks-begin-with-spear-phishing-email/ [accessed on 2.17.2014].

CHAPTER 12

Bringing It All Together

Valerie Thomas
Securicon, Lorton, VA, USA

We've covered the building blocks of an awareness program in the previous chapters. Now, we'll explore some examples of using those building blocks to construct a complete program. The sample plans discussed are meant to provide you with a program baseline and can be tailored to fit the needs of your organization.

CREATE A SECURITY AWARENESS WEBSITE

This website should be the face of your awareness program. It should provide employees with a trusted resource for up-to-date information. Nobody wants to search through their e-mail for policies or procedures, especially when the website provides them with all of the resources they need [1]. At a minimum, content should include

- e-mail address and phone number for reporting suspicious activity
- training and reference material
- alerts for recently received phishing e-mails or phone calls
- corporate policies on computer use and physical security
- antivirus information for their home computer
- security tip of the day
- links to external articles on popular topics, such as identity theft

In addition to containing useful information, the awareness website also needs to be engaging to encourage employees to visit. Attention-grabbing headlines, topics, and graphics hold the reader's attention to the topic at hand [2]. Including short security videos [3] or cartoons [4] create an attractive and education website. Work with your marketing and web development teams to streamline the visitor's experience. Most importantly, website content must be current to entice employees to visit frequently. Although you will want the website to be full of useful content, do not overload with extraneous material, as some employees will not be able to distinguish useful information from general information.

SAMPLE PLANS

Low Budget

This plan is best suited for an organization with a limited budget. If divisions are geographically dispersed, the in-person training portions can either be presented by a local security contact or be recorded from a presentation at the main corporate office.

New Hire Training

- In-person lecture style to cover corporate policies of the following:
  - Data classification
  - Authorized computer use
  - Physical entry and exit procedures
  - Handling sensitive information
  - Reporting suspicious e-mails or activities
  - Regulatory-specific requires (if applicable)
- Computer-based training (CBT), web-based training (WBT), or video training for the following:
  - Computer/laptop safety
  - Phishing awareness and prevention basics
  - Good security habits
  - Safe web browsing
  - Choosing effective passwords
  - Social engineering

Many free sources exist for CBT, WBT, and video training. See Chapter 8 for examples of free and commercial training products. One form of CBT can also be a slideshow produced by your security team. If you select a solution without progress tracking, ensure that a method for tracking when each employee has completed training is determined.

Biannual Training

The majority of biannual training reiterates the fundamentals covered in new hire training, but with a few additional topics.

Use the CBT, WBT, or video training modules from new hire training. Content should also be added to include

- security-related policy or procedure changes
- review of physical security basics, such as tailgating

- visitor policy
- reporting procedures of suspicious e-mails and/or activities
- handling of sensitive information
- removable media safety
- new security-related software, such as a password safe

Continual Training

Posters are one of the least expensive awareness resources available. The two largest factors in successfully utilizing posters are location and content. Place poster in high-traffic areas where they have the most visibility. Also, rotate the posters, both content and location placement to ensure that staff is continually reviewing the material. In doing this, you have a greater chance of staff members retaining the information on the posters. Additional information on posters is available in Chapter 8. Other methods of keeping information fresh for staff member are to continually update the security awareness website and publish a monthly or quarterly newsletter on various security-related topics. These are effective ways of keeping security on the minds of employees.

A homemade video campaign is another low-cost training option. Videos should be informal—think more YouTube and less Hollywood—and only a minute or two long. Featuring employees in the video encourages everyone to participate. Introducing some humor in your videos can also encourage staff often to look forward to watching them, as it inspires camaraderie and helps staff relate to a topic. Also include a "suggestion box" e-mail account for employees to submit ideas for future content.

Many no-cost options exist for lunch and learn sessions. Security team or other staff members (under guidance and approval from the security team) can author session content for presentations. Speaking at these events is also a good way for those who wish to improve their public speaking skills. Another option is to watch a short video and hold a group discussion afterward. Begin with quarterly sessions, and add sessions based on popularity and volunteer presenters. Some examples of lunch and learn topics can be found in Chapter 8.

Phishing Assessment

Organizations should aim to complete a minimum of two phishing assessments per year. Open-source software is the cheapest option for implementing your own phishing assessment. The Social Engineering Toolkit (SET), as discussed in Chapter 10, is a free tool for performing your own phishing assessment. SET requires basic Linux and Apache knowledge, so this task is best assigned to a technically skilled member of the security team. Ensure that results are stored in a spreadsheet or similar format for long-term tracking and comparison.

Moderate Budget

This plan is best suited for an organization with a moderate budget and assumes that locations are geographically dispersed. The focus of this plan is to utilize funding in areas with the greatest benefit of process automation and content. The in-person training portions can either be presented by a local security contact or be recorded from a presentation at the main corporate office. The in-person training portions of the program are designed to put a face to the security group or local contact in the organization.

New Hire Training

- In-person lecture style to cover corporate policies of the following:
  - Data classification
  - Authorized computer use
  - Physical entry and exit procedures
  - Handling sensitive information
  - Reporting suspicious e-mails or activities
  - Regulatory-specific requires (if applicable)
- CBT, WBT, or video training for the following:
  - Computer/laptop safety
  - Phishing awareness and prevention basics
  - Good security habits
  - Safe web browsing
  - Choosing effective passwords
  - Social engineering

For moderate budgets, the best option is a commercial solution WBT that has stand-alone training modules, phishing assessment capabilities, training modules that can be combined with a failed phishing assessment, and progress tracking. Progress tracking should include when employees have taken the required training and results from phishing assessments.

Biannual Training

The majority of biannual training reiterates the fundamentals covered in new hire training, but with a few additional topics. Utilize the WBT modules from new hire training. Content should also be added to include

- security-related policy or procedure changes
- review of physical security basics, such as tailgating
- visitor policy
- reporting procedures of suspicious e-mails and/or activities
- handling sensitive information
- removable of media safety
- new security-related software, such as a password safe

Keep in mind that biannual training sessions are not required to use the same delivery method. For instance, the first training session of the year could be WBT, and the second training session could be an in-person presentation. Changing delivery methods is often a good way to aid staff in data retention and overall awareness.

Continual Training

The first priority of funds should be for a robust commercial solution that integrates training, phishing, and tracking abilities. If additional funding is available, consider adding a commercial video campaign to your awareness program. Restricted Intelligence offers a comedy-based approach with a video series that teaches security basics with an entertaining twist. The campaign takes an approach similar to a television series where videos are released one at a time. Packages include posters, teaser video clips, and other resources to advertise the video series. More information can be found at http://www.restrictedintelligence.co.uk/.

Posters are one of the most popular and least expensive awareness resources available. The two largest factors in successfully utilizing posters are location and content. Place poster in high-traffic areas where they have the most visibility. Also, rotate the posters, both content and location placement to ensure that staff is continually reviewing the material. In doing this, you have a greater chance of staff members retaining the information on the posters. Additional information on posters is available in Chapter 8. Other methods of keeping information fresh for staff member are to continually update the security awareness website and publish a monthly or quarterly newsletter on various security-related topics. These are effective way of keeping security on the minds of employees.

Lunch and learn sessions can also be incorporated into your awareness program, but should not use much of the annual program budget. Many no-cost and low-cost options exist for lunch and learn sessions. Security team or other staff members (under guidance and approval from the security team) can author session content for presentations. Speaking at these events is also a good way for those who wish to improve their public speaking skills. Some examples of lunch and learn topics can be found in Chapter 8.

Phishing Assessment

If you've invested in a robust commercial solution that includes phishing assessment capability along with training, phishing assessments should be completed quarterly. Develop an assessment schedule for each quarter to review with the contact list as discussed in Chapter 10. If your organization is small to medium, it may be possible to perform phishing assessments on a monthly basis. By including training for those who fail the phishing assessment, you're delivering a year-round training program that reinforces material delivered in the biannual training sessions.

Large Budget

If your organization is fortunate enough to have a large budget, the following plan should serve as a baseline for minimal activities. The plan assumes the organization has a large number of employees that are geographically dispersed and must meet regulatory training requirements. The focus of this plan is to utilize funding in areas with the greatest benefit of process automation and content. While in-person training portions work well for some organizations, more technology-based delivery solutions may fit best for a large number of employees.

New Hire Training
- CBT, WBT, or video training for the following:
  - Data classification
  - Authorized computer use
  - Physical entry and exit procedures
  - Handling of sensitive information
  - Reporting procedures of suspicious e-mails and/or activities
  - Regulatory-specific requires (if applicable)
  - Computer/laptop safety
  - Phishing awareness and prevention basics
  - Good security habits
  - Safe web browsing
  - Choosing effective passwords
  - Social engineering

For organization-specific topics, a custom WBT solution is optimal. Custom WBT solutions with long-term support enable you to specify required content with the ability to update the material over time. Due to the potentially sensitive material, it is best to host the WBT inside your environment. When selecting a commercial product, ensure that the content can be hosted in your environment.

For the general security topics, invest in a WBT that has stand-alone training modules, phishing assessment capabilities, training modules that can be combined with a failed phishing assessment, and progress tracking. Progress tracking should include when employees have taken the required training and results from phishing assessments.

Biannual Training

The majority of biannual training reiterates the fundamentals covered in new hire training, but with a few additional topics. Utilize the WBT modules from new hire training. Content should also be added to include

- security-related policy or procedure changes
- review of physical security basics, such as tailgating
- visitor policy
- reporting procedures of suspicious e-mails and/or activities
- handling of sensitive information
- removable media safety
- new security-related software, such as a password safe

Keep in mind that biannual training sessions are not required to use the same delivery method. For instance, the first training session of the year could be WBT, and the second training session could be an in-person presentation. While recording an in-person presentation for remote locations is an option, for maximum effect, the local on-site security manager should present the material. This provides employees the opportunity to ask questions in person and become familiar with the local security team.

Continual Training

The first priority of funds should be for a robust commercial solution that integrates training, phishing, and tracking abilities. If additional funding is available, consider adding a commercial video campaign to your awareness program. Commercial video campaigns are ideal for large organizations because they provide continual security awareness. Restricted Intelligence offers a comedy-based approach with a video series that teaches security basics with an entertaining twist. The campaign takes an approach similar to a television series where videos are released one at a time. Packages include posters, teaser video clips, and other resources to advertise the video series. More information can be found at http://www.restrictedintelligence.co.uk/.

Even though posters are considered a low-cost awareness resource, they should still be incorporated into your awareness program. In large organizations, it's unlikely that employees will have day-to-day interaction with the security team. Posters are used to provide employees with subtle reminders of best security practices. If you invest in a commercial video campaign, posters are often included in the purchase price. Additional information on posters is available in Chapter 8. In addition to updating the security awareness website, publishing a monthly or quarterly newsletter on various security-related topics is an effective way of keeping security on the minds of employees.

For large organizations, lunch and learn sessions can be logistically challenging, but not impossible. Sessions that are hosted at the headquarters facility can be recorded or broadcast live with video teleconference software. Additionally, remote locations can host local sessions. Security team or other staff members (under guidance and approval from the security team) can author session content for presentations. Speaking at these events is also a good way for those who wish to improve their public speaking skills. If the budget allows, consider hiring a popular speaking figure to encourage attendance. Examples of lunch and learn topics can be found in Chapter 8.

Phishing Assessment

Phishing assessments should be completed quarterly with a robust commercial solution that includes phishing assessment capability along with training. Develop an assessment schedule for each quarter to review with the contact list as discussed in Chapter 10. By including training for those who fail the phishing assessment, you're delivering a year-round training program that reinforces material delivered in the biannual training sessions.

PROMOTING YOUR AWARENESS PROGRAM

All awareness programs need to be promoted in order to be successful. However, getting employees involved isn't always an easy task. It may often require marketing your program internally, also known as social engineering your own (staff). Not only are you promoting an awareness program, but also you're influencing a security-aware culture. Here are some activities to get you started.

Contests and Prizes

People are competitive by nature, and even more so when some type of prize is involved. Contests are a great way to get everyone's attention and participation. Here are some examples to get you started:

- Prizes for correct answers to security questions based on procedure, compliance, or any other presented material
- Security poster contest
- Prize or recognition for those with perfect phishing assessment scores
- Homemade awareness video contest
- Monthly drawing for those who report potential phishing

Prizes can vary in accordance with your budget. However, prizes don't always need to be expensive to effective. Some popular options are

- gift cards
- movie passes
- event tickets

- reserved parking space
- cash
- small electronic devices, such as MP3 players

Announcements

Implementing a monthly security e-mail campaign can keep your employees up-to-date and increase traffic to your security awareness website. Short, monthly e-mails should contain one key message. Also include links to new material on the security awareness website. Positive public recognition can be a powerful tool for employee motivation. Consider featuring an employee who reported suspicious activity or other security-conscience behavior.

National Cyber Security Awareness Month

Created by the US Department of Homeland Security and the National Cyber Security Alliance, National Cyber Security Awareness Month (NCSAM) is observed in October. NCSAM is designed to create a safe cyber environment across government and civilian organizations [5]. NCSAM can be used to reinforce previously taught material, as well as introduce new content. It is common to declare a theme for each week, but is not required. Some sample themes include the following:

- Security: A shared responsibility
- Mobile security
- Identity theft
- Dangers of social media
- Keeping children safe online
- Cyber crime

NCSAM events can vary from special edition desktop backgrounds to a cyber security fair with presentations and activities. Many universities and organizations provide free material for NCSAM planning and coordination. Information is also available at http://www.staysafeonline.org/ncsam/.

Notes

[1] Security Awareness Quick Start Guide https://wiki.internet2.edu/confluence/display/itsg2/Security+Awareness+Quick+Start+Guide [accessed on 3.16.2014].

[2] Developing Your Campus Information Security Website https://wiki.internet2.edu/confluence/display/itsg2/Developing+Your+Campus+Information+Security+Website [accessed on 3.16.2014].

[3] Federal Trade Commission Consumer Information http://www.consumer.ftc.gov/media [accessed on 3.16.2014].

[4] Security Cartoons http://www.securitycartoon.com/ [accessed on 3.16.2014].

[5] Nation Cyber Security Awareness Month http://www.dhs.gov/national-cyber-security-awareness-month [accessed on 3.22.2014].

CHAPTER 13

Measuring Effectiveness

Valerie Thomas
Securicon, Lorton, VA, USA

MEASURING EFFECTIVENESS

An often forgotten part of an awareness program is a method of tracking progress and measuring impact. These metrics are to be used as a guide for making adjustments to the program and reporting progress to senior management. If your organization has a risk management team, consult with them on their current metrics program. It's likely that a portion of their collected data could be used for awareness training metrics.

MEASUREMENTS VS. METRICS

These information types are often used interchangeably; however, they are not the same.

A measurement is a value determined at a specific time that is generated by counting [1]. An example of a measurement is the number of infected computers reported last month.

Metrics are generated by the analysis of measurements. A metric is a comparison of two or more measurements taken over a certain amount of time and compared to a predetermined baseline [1]. For example, the number of infected computers increased by 5% in the second quarter from the first quarter. Useable metrics are dependent on accurate measurements.

CREATING METRICS

Successful metrics programs include well-defined measurements and the necessary steps to obtain them. Documentation of required measurements and responsible individuals is key. The following example is from the SANS community website [2]. Many awareness program resources are available, including a sample metrics matrix at https://www.securingthehuman.org/resources/security-awareness-roadmap/. Each metric should have the following segments at minimum.

Metric Name

The metric name should be a high-level topic that can be calculated from one or more types of measurements. For this example, we'll use phishing detection.

What is Measured

Measurements are objective raw data, meaning no human interpretation is required to obtain the measurement value. A measurement for phishing detection is the number of suspicious e-mails reported to the security team. This measurement is designed to evaluate the number of employees who followed the proper procedure for reporting suspicious messages. While this measurement alone is sufficient, an additional measurement can provide more insight. Measuring the number of help desk calls or e-mails about suspicious e-mail can also be useful, as it can indicate the number of employees who did not follow the proper procedure.

There is no limit on the number of measurements that can be collected. Some additional measurements for phishing detection associated with an assessment are

- number of e-mails sent
- number of e-mails opened
- number of employees that clicked the link
- number of employees that entered information

How it's Measured

A common way to obtain phishing detection measurements is to perform an assessment. To continue with the phishing detection example, a measurement of how many suspicious e-mails were reported to security would be collected at the end of each phishing assessment (Figure 13.1). If you're using a commercial tool, the number of e-mails sent during each assessment is available from the reporting screen.

When it's Measured

Phishing exercise measurements should be obtained at the end of each assessment. If your organization performs biannual assessments, then collect the data biannually. However, not all reported e-mails are assessment-related. Therefore, nonassessment data should be collected on a monthly basis.

[export] ⤓ Save as pdf

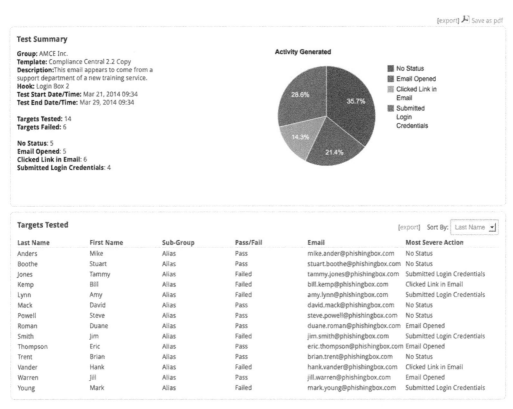

Test Summary

Group: AMCE Inc.
Template: Compliance Central 2.2 Copy
Description: This email appears to come from a
support department of a new training service.
Hook: Login Box 2
Test Start Date/Time: Mar 21, 2014 09:34
Test End Date/Time: Mar 29, 2014 09:34

Targets Tested: 14
Targets Failed: 6

No Status: 5
Email Opened: 5
Clicked Link in Email: 6
Submitted Login Credentials: 4

Activity Generated

- No Status
- Email Opened
- Clicked Link in Email
- Submitted Login Credentials

35.7% 28.6% 14.3% 21.4%

Targets Tested   [export] Sort By: Last Name ▼

Last Name	First Name	Sub-Group	Pass/Fail	Email	Most Severe Action
Anders	Mike	Alias	Pass	mike.ander@phishingbox.com	No Status
Boothe	Stuart	Alias	Pass	stuart.boothe@phishingbox.com	No Status
Jones	Tammy	Alias	Failed	tammy.jones@phishingbox.com	Submitted Login Credentials
Kemp	Bill	Alias	Failed	bill.kemp@phishingbox.com	Clicked Link in Email
Lynn	Amy	Alias	Failed	amy.lynn@phishingbox.com	Submitted Login Credentials
Mack	David	Alias	Pass	david.mack@phishingbox.com	No Status
Powell	Steve	Alias	Pass	steve.powell@phishingbox.com	No Status
Roman	Duane	Alias	Pass	duane.roman@phishingbox.com	Email Opened
Smith	Jim	Alias	Failed	jim.smith@phishingbox.com	Submitted Login Credentials
Thompson	Eric	Alias	Pass	eric.thompson@phishingbox.com	Email Opened
Trent	Brian	Alias	Pass	brian.trent@phishingbox.com	No Status
Vander	Hank	Alias	Failed	hank.vander@phishingbox.com	Clicked Link in Email
Warren	Jill	Alias	Pass	jill.warren@phishingbox.com	Email Opened
Young	Mark	Alias	Failed	mark.young@phishingbox.com	Submitted Login Credentials

FIGURE 13.1 Reporting menu of PhishingBox.

Who Measures

Multiple information sources exist for this metric. The security team collects the
number of suspicious e-mails received. Phishing assessment-related data are
collected by the assessment point of contact. The help desk collects the number
of e-mails and phone calls received in reference to phishing e-mails.

ADDITIONAL MEASUREMENTS

Now that we've covered an example, here are some other useful measurements:

- Number of infected machines
- Number of employees that have completed awareness training
- Number of lunch and learn attendees
- Number of hits on the security awareness website
- Number of general questions e-mailed to the security group

- Employee test scores throughout the year
- Number of sensitive documents left in public areas
- Number of unattended computers that are unlocked
- Number of employees wearing their badges outside the building

If your awareness program is new, it's likely your measurements will focus more on deployment. Even if your awareness program isn't fully implemented, collecting operational measurements is important to demonstrate improvement over time.

REPORTING METRICS

Metrics are designed to provide viewers with the information they need to make decisions. However, if the metrics are presented incorrectly, they will be considered ineffective and reflect poorly on the awareness program. The secret to properly presenting metrics is understanding the target audience.

One popular presentation style is the tiered approach [3]. At the top tier, senior management is interested in high-level information that provides insight into program maturity, cost, and benefits. It's essential to show that the awareness program is having a positive impact on the overall security culture of the organization. The middle tier, middle management, requires information at a department level to evaluate performance levels and potential business impact. The lowest tier consists of awareness program managers and personnel. This tier requires detailed information in order to adjust program content for better performance.

Building Your Presentation

Once your audience has been determined and appropriate metrics selected, it's time to build your presentation. Some key elements of presenting metrics are the following:

Introduction
Provide a short introduction of the program. If the program is in deployment, provide a brief synopsis of the deployment plan, key milestones, and achievements to date.

How Metrics were Derived
Explain at a high level what measurements were obtained and how they were collected. Time is an essential factor for decision-making, so include how often measurements were obtained as well.

The Metrics

As discussed above, only include metrics that are relevant to your audience. Charts are the most popular style of metric reporting. However, a chart is only useful if it depicts the data in a meaningful way. Selecting the correct type of chart for you data is essential. The three main categories of charts are comparison, transition, and composition [4].

Comparison charts are best for identifying highs and lows of numbers. The number of reported suspicious e-mails per quarter over a two-year period is best represented in this format (Figure 13.2). Clustered bar charts and column charts are the most popular representations.

Transition charts are ideal for time-based data to understand the rate of change. The number of visits to the security awareness website and the number of employees who fell prey to a phishing exercise are both excellent candidates for a transition chart (Figure 13.3). Line and area charts are best suited to represent this type of data.

Composition charts represent how a data value breaks down into segments. Awareness training completed by each department is best represented as a composition chart. Many phishing assessment details can also be presented this way. The percentage of employees that opened a phishing e-mail, the percentage of employees that clicked the enclosed link, and the percentage of employees that did not open the e-mail can be represented in a composition chart (Figure 13.4). Pie charts are the most popular representation of this type of data; however, a stacked bar chart can also be utilized.

Use basic colors that are easy to see in color and gray scale. While vibrant color choices are tempting, they are often difficult to see if projected. Above all, keep

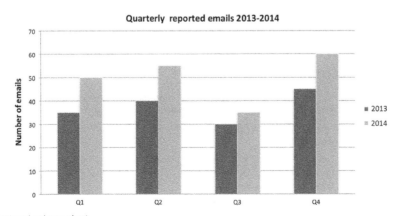

FIGURE 13.2 Clustered column chart.

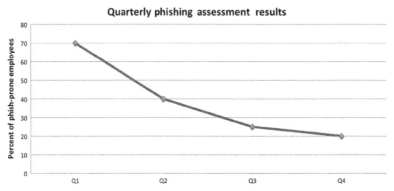

FIGURE 13.3 Line chart with data points.

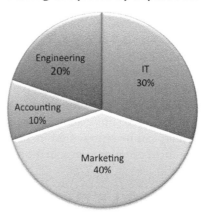

FIGURE 13.4 Pie chart with percentages.

slides and report sections simple. One slide should discuss one subject only. Mixing subjects and metrics on a slide often distracts the viewer, making the presentation difficult to understand.

Notes

[1] Guide To Security Metrics http://www.docstoc.com/docs/7264928/Guide-to-Security-Metrics-SHIRLEY-C-PAYNE-DIRECTOR-IT/.

[2] Security Awareness Roadmap https://www.securingthehuman.org/resources/security-awareness-roadmap/.

[3] Developing Metrics for Effective Information Security Governance http://www.isaca.org/Journal/Past-Issues/2007/Volume-2/Pages/Developing-Metrics-for-Effective-Information-Security-Governance1.aspx.

[4] Selecting the Right Chart Type for your Data, http://www.tutorial9.net/tutorials/web-tutorials/selecting-the-right-chart-type-for-your-data/.

CHAPTER 14

Stories from the Front Lines

Bill Gardner
Marshall University, Huntington, WV, USA

We asked information security professionals about their experience in building their own information security awareness programs and here is what they had to say.

PHIL GRIMES

Phil Grimes is a parent, a biker, and an information security professional with experience in providing security assessments and penetration testing services to organizations ranging from small businesses, financial institutions, eCommerce, telecommunications, manufacturing, education and government agencies, and international corporations. Phil started learning networking and Internet security as a hobby harassing AOL in 1996, developing his technical skill set independently until joining the professional security industry in 2009. After a change in his career trajectory in 2012, vulnerability research and exploit development became the main focus of attention. Phil's experience in application security, penetration testing, mobile/smartphone security, and social engineering has proven successful in assessments for high-profile customers both domestically and around the globe. An accomplished speaker and presenter, Phil has engaged on various topics for Notacon, for CUISPA conferences, and at the Central Ohio ISSA InfoSec Summit in addition to various other speaking appearances to a wide range of audiences.

Q: Thanks for taking part in this Q&A. Please tell us about yourself.

A: I'm an independent security researcher with focus on vulnerability research and exploit development, mainly targeting Web applications and humans. I've been involved in the "hacking scene" since the mid-1990s and have always had a passion for breaking systems, whatever they might be. I broke into information security in 2009 but took a break in 2013 to resume my independent research work. I've spoken to technical and managerial audiences around the country on a wide variety of topics aimed at user awareness and educations as well as demonstrations about how various attacks are carried out.

Q: What constitutes an information security awareness program in your opinion?

A: In order for a security awareness plan to work, it has to engage the employees. There has to be some reason for the individual to "buy in" and this usually goes beyond work. Correlating security issues to the user's daily lives will put the risk into terms that they understand and help them to realize how all facets of our technical lives intertwine with many parts of our physical lives inadvertently. Encouraging the people to police themselves (and each other) and to reward those who speak out when things aren't right will help change the culture from one of complacent silence to one of engaged interaction.

Q: Why are social engineering and other nontechnical attacks so successful?

A: Humans are the weakest link in computing and business. Understanding that, attackers leverage devastating attacks on the human element within an organization by understanding psychology then using normal human behavior and societal norms to get people to do things that they shouldn't or wouldn't normally do. Combined with technical attacks, and an endless combination of the two, the organization finds itself fighting a constant uphill battle where they must be "right" every day to succeed and being "wrong" only once could cripple or destroy it completely.

Q: How do you get management buy-in for a program?

A: Here's the million-dollar question. The fact is that the only way to accomplish this is to show them the fallout that can/will result from NOT making progress in this arena. Security is always treated as the stepchild and isn't made a priority by the decision makers until after it's too late. Part of the awareness program has to be testing our users. Oftentimes, that has to be the first component and has to be leveraged before any plans are formalized because it provides metrics and allows tangible proof to be given to management in support of why we need to make this a priority.

Q: What are the biggest challenges to building an information security awareness program for organizations?

A: Getting management buy-in.

Q: Is budget an issue?

A: Yes, but it doesn't need to be. One hour, once or twice a quarter for meetings, and give the security team the ability to test the users, analyze the results, and correlate this data to what's presented at the meetings. There doesn't need to be a huge budget for this.

Q: What were the political obstacles that needed to be overcome?

A: This ties into the previous questions. Getting the buy-in from management and overcoming the budgetary objections lay the foundation for this. There is always the element of interpersonal relationships within the organization that must be considered. Politics is an ugly side effect of being in business and this must be considered when creating the security awareness plan.

Q: What metrics are useful for measuring the success of an information security awareness program?

A: We test our users by implementing various controlled attacks against them and get a dataset that allows us to gauge the various metrics that we'll use to tailor the awareness program. Things like "we sent 100 e-mails and 30 were opened, 18 clicked the malicious link inside, and 3 reported it as suspicious." Being able to create situations that allow our security teams to formulate these statements will allow for the security awareness program to be targeted toward the relevant threat and allow us to create a program based around rational response.

Q: What failures and pitfall did you encounter in information security awareness programs?

A: Lack of consistency, lack of metrics, lack of follow-through, lack of policy, lack of enforcement, lack of importance placed upon the program.

Q: What were the successes you encountered in information security awareness programs?

A: I've conducted user awareness sessions for a particular client for several years running and it's been really fulfilling to see familiar faces come up and recite something they've learned in my session or to have them engage me and/or each other during (and even after) my sessions to talk about how they've done things differently. It's been a great success to see them change their way of thinking.

Q: What is the best training cycle for a program?

A: I believe quarterly is adequately if the program is comprehensive. This keeps the material fresh in their heads and makes it something that's always on the back burner.

Q: What learning and teaching styles work the best?

A: I don't think this is something one person can answer. How I teach may not work for someone else. How I learn certainly wouldn't. In creating a program that is targeting a wide range of individuals, I've seen success with several schools of thought. Beat it into their heads over and over again, which is tedious and expensive. Make a "conference-style" day of it to allow for different sessions that employ different techniques so the people can experience different flavors and find what suits them. I've also seen several styles wrapped into one where the audience listened, spoke, read, and participated in various segments throughout the program. I believe getting feedback from the audience is important because the security awareness program must be a living, breathing, dynamic beast that constantly evolves to meet the needs of both the business and the individuals.

Q: What is your advice for others building their own programs?

A: Just do it. If you're already doing it, keep doing it. As long as we're trying, that's better than doing nothing. Be happy with baby steps but don't accept complacency.

Q: What is the advantage of building your own program over buying a prebuilt information security awareness program from a vendor?

A: There is no "silver bullet." While there is a framework for this as with anything, the war is won and lost in the details. Using this framework is great but there is a lot of introspection that an organization must perform when using these frameworks to build a program. Anything less is simply lulling the organization into a false sense of security.

Q: Is there anything we haven't covered that you would like to add?

A: Building a security awareness program is vital to every organization. Your people are your best investment and can be more valuable than any IDS/IPS, any firewall, and any antivirus you can purchase. But like any security tool, they must be tested and tuned regularly.

AMANDA BERLIN

Amanda Berlin is a network analyst at a regional medical center in northern Ohio. She has recently changed focus to information security-related topics. She manages the internal phishing campaign at her company to promote user education about phishing and hacking through an award-based reporting program, as well as having other system administration-related and network administration-related responsibilities.

Q: Thanks for taking part in this Q&A. Please tell us about yourself.

A: My name is Amanda Berlin, and I work for a medium-size medical center in Ohio. I've been in IT for approximately 10 years and a part of the networking team in our organization for 4 years (2010). Our network team is in charge of the organization's infrastructure and security. I've always been interested in security and just recently have had the opportunity to become more active in the information security community and start on a path to becoming a penetration tester. I'm also the lead and major contributor of our information security awareness program called "Something Smells Phishy." In this program, our users are subjugated monthly to targeted phishing e-mails with malicious links or attachments.

Q: What constitutes an information security awareness program in your opinion?

A: One that works to reduce the likelihood of employees introducing threats into an environment. Only one click on a phishing e-mail can compromise your environment and the weakest link is the human element. The program should slowly start at the basics, like not clicking on suspicious links/attachments in e-mails and learning what constitutes as suspicious. Then, build up to things like pretexting, tailgating, USB drive drops, and more advanced techniques.

It should contain easy-to-read, concise content that will engage and entertain the audience as well as a reward system to encourage the users to act upon the information they have learned. It needs to be encouraging to the users as well as memorable. No one wants to feel like you are talking down to them because they should have known better. It's our job to show them what they need to know to get by. Each occupation has their own specialty; we need to remember not to expect them to know the ins and outs of information security. Just like we're not required to know the same about what they do every day. Positive reinforcement will go a long way in making what you say stick with them.

Having the ability to adapt and grow with the changes in your environment and with the advancements of the threat landscape when planned and executed properly can save a lot of time and headache.

Q: What was the reason for building your own program?

A: There were several reasons we made this decision. The first and most obvious was to increase our security posture through education. We knew that no training had been put in place before in our organization. Many of us had seen firsthand how little our employees knew about the best practices with anything security-related.

Another driving factor was that we thought it wouldn't be too difficult to do at a low cost. With the talent that we have on staff, we were willing to take a chance and see how much of an improvement we could make. We were approved for

$1000 worth of prizes for our awards. This money was split up into different denomination gift cards to be used as prizes for users that would report phishing attempts. This amount when compared to already established security awareness programs is a huge cost savings.

Q: How did you get management buy-in for your program?

A: I am extremely lucky to have such security conscience management. Our CEO is a former CIO, and the entire leadership team understands how important information security is. One major turning point was the result of our 2013 penetration test where several employees were successfully phished that resulted in the exploitation of our network. We were able to show them the low cost of what we believed would majorly improve our chances to mitigate these attacks.

Q: What was your biggest challenge to building an information security awareness program for your organization?

A: So far, there have been two major challenges. The most outward-facing would be the notification to the employees about the program. In my opinion, we didn't go far enough with spreading the word on what the point of the entire program was. This was the one area that was weak with management buy-in. I feel that we had the means to spread word of the program in several fashions and was denied the opportunity. Once several high-ranking individuals were successfully phished, more chances presented themselves, giving me access to reach more people by different media.

The second and more inner-facing issue is mining the data. We have over 2000 mailboxes on our exchange server. While I've used PowerShell to strip out a list of accounts to target, having to manually merge that with the SET xml and keep track of that in a spreadsheet is not fun. My idea is to have a python script with a MySQL backend to parse the data from the xml, pull in data live from Microsoft AD, and report.

Q: Was budget an issue?

A: Nope.

Q: What were the political obstacles that needed to be overcome?

A: We didn't have any major political obstacles. Of the few minor issues we had, one was some of the older employees felt like we were trying to get them in trouble. We had one notorious complainer let us know that she'd never trust our department again. I also sent out a phishing campaign that was a spoof of an Amazon receipt. It caused one of our employees to call Kohl's and cancel their credit card as well as call PayPal and start a fraud claim. As a measure of good faith, we gave that particular user a gift card as well.

Q: What metrics are useful for measuring the success of an information security awareness program?

A: We are using the difference in reporting over time from phishing e-mails, legitimate both from external sources and from our internal campaigns. Before starting this campaign, we would rarely get reports of suspicious-looking e-mails, computer activity, or Web sites. We now get them daily and have been able to take reactionary and proactive steps to block and report e-mails that have made it through our spam filtering.

The metrics we are currently using are percentage of links clicked per campaign, percentage of user/pass given up per campaign, and percentage of reports monthly.

Q: What failures and pitfall did you encounter in building an information security awareness program?

A: I think so far the only failures would be the lack of reach of the program details to our users as well as my personal failures when running campaigns. I personally liked hitting them with the element of surprise. I wanted to see what our level of exposure was without any prior warning or training. However, others thought that we might have been better off pounding the program into people's heads before running them. While a difference of opinion, I still think it's a pitfall.

As far as my personal failures go, in the beginning, I had a couple of occurrences where SET didn't do exactly what I had expected. This made me have to rerun the campaign quickly while people were trying to log in. I think I would have gotten higher numbers of clicks and log-ins if I had made sure to test more beforehand.

Q: What is the best training cycle for a program?

A:

1. Phish.
2. Educate—right after being phished and the entire user population (posters, e-mails, PowerPoint, videos, etc.).
3. Repeat—with a more advanced campaign. Make sure to include repeat offenders each time until they make a report.

It's my thought that the repetitive process of phishing to grab their attention, and then teaching them what they did wrong, is a great way to make the training stick. There's nothing like a mistake or getting your hand caught in the cookie jar to leave a lasting impression.

Q: What learning and teaching styles did you use for your program?

A: We set our program up to be able to grow with the speed at which our employees learned. Starting out slow, I used theHarvester.py to get as many e-mails from the Web for our organization. This allowed us to attack the most likely candidates that someone without inside access would be able to discover. After that, I progressed to the most used mailboxes and then a random sampling of everyone. If a user clicked and gave up their password, they were automatically redirected to a PowerPoint slide on what phishing actually is, how it can hurt us, and what they can do to help.

We also have training modules created on a variety of topics to help users learn to be more secure. These modules are lumped in with our other required learning for the year as an employee, always with an emphasis on reporting suspicious behavior.

Q: What is the advantage of building your own program over buying a prebuilt information security awareness program from a vendor?

A: Overall, the cost and the ability to customize the program to easily fit your organization's needs.

Q: What were the successes you encountered in building an information security awareness program?

A: There was overwhelming positive feedback and encouragement from our employees. I had several people joke with me about it as well as asking questions and starting discussions about information security. I've had individual departments reach out to me to do some smaller training sessions.

Also, there has been a huge improvement in our employee's security knowledge and reporting skills. The amount of reports of legitimate outside phishing attempts has skyrocketed. We went from 36% successful internal phish rate down to an 11% and then to a 1%. While the first three months were all the same type of campaign, I still consider it a successful metric.

Q: What advice do you have for people who are currently building their own information security awareness programs?

A:

1. Plan everything out in as much detail as you can. It would be nice to have a good 6 months or even a year of ideas set aside if you plan on actively phishing users.
2. Know what you are trying to accomplish.
3. Try to identify potential pitfalls and make sure you have good responses.
4. If you have a help desk or several groups of people that will be contacted about your program, make sure that they project a unified view of the expectations of users as well as the positives of the entire process.

5. Make it into a game or contest. People love winning things, especially if they have a good chance at it. Make sure the game/contest rules are explicitly set beforehand as well.

Q: Is there anything we haven't covered that you would like to add?

A: For me, this project not only has been a lot of fun but also has been an amazing learning experience. For someone just starting to become active in the information security community, this was a great first step. Being on both the red and blue team side is a great place to be. You can figure out where your company's weaknesses are and then take active steps to mitigate them. I encourage everyone as a network or system administrator to take the steps to begin one of these programs in your company. No matter how big or how small, we all need to take steps at making businesses more secure.

JIMMY VO

Jimmy Vo is a security consultant in a firm based in southeast Michigan. Prior to being a security consultant, he was a security and systems analyst for an organization in the financial sector. His focuses are security monitoring and security assessments. He is an active member of OWASP Detroit and MiSec. Jimmy holds a master's degree from Boston University in Computer Information Systems.

Q: Thanks for taking part in this Q&A. Please tell us about yourself.

A: I'm currently working as a security consultant in a firm based in Michigan. My current role with security awareness however is the same as my last job. At my prior job, I was the lone "security" guy among other many other roles for a small company.

Q: What constitutes an information security awareness program in your opinion?

A: In my opinion, security awareness is just like a business function. It must support the company goals and deliver value. The value is getting coworkers to care about security and not look at it like an annoyance. A security awareness program can vary based on the organization but key components would include metrics that matter, delivering awareness material and evaluating effectiveness.

Q: What was the reason for building your own program?

A: There were two main reasons why I decided to build a security awareness program at my previous job:

(1) Spear phishing was becoming more and more used.
(2) Security awareness in my mind is building culture. I was trying to build a security program at the time, and the first part of it was to build a culture around security. Security awareness program addressed this.

Q: How did you get management buy-in for your program?

A: Management buy-in was very simple since I did not have to procure thousand-dollar appliances. It was a time investment, which I had a little to spare (or I thought). The executive team took security very seriously due to the business they were in.

Q: What was your biggest challenge to building an information security awareness program for your organization?

A: The biggest challenge was being consistent. I was on a very small team responsible for many other functions in the business. It took time and planning to manage the program, and there were times where the time was not available. Prioritizing delivering projects versus focusing on security awareness was pretty simple. Delivering projects brought income; security awareness did not have a direct ROI. That was a huge challenge.

Q: Was budget an issue?

A: Budget was not an issue, it was just time.

Q: What were the political obstacles that needed to be overcome?

A: No political obstacles in getting the program started.

Q: What metrics are useful for measuring the success of an information security awareness program?

A: The only metric that was used was the numbers of phishing attempts reported. It didn't measure much; however, it was data.

Q: What failures and pitfall did you encounter in building an information security awareness program?

A: The biggest pitfall/failure was the lack of experience in building a security awareness program. The other was related to the challenge of lack of time.

Q: What is the best training cycle for a program?

A: I think the training cycle is relative to your organization: My organization shows great disparity in generations and learning styles.

Q: What learning and teaching styles did you use for your program?

A: Since the awareness program was very young and I left the organization shortly after it was made, I used monthly newsletters with useful information.

Q: What is your advice for others building their own programs?

A: My advice would be to see it through and stick with it. If you don't have the time, make the time. Also remember some awareness is better than no awareness. It doesn't have to be a perfect program at first.

Q: What is the advantage of building your own program over buying a prebuilt information security awareness program from a vendor?

A: The advantage is cost savings. However, quality can suffer if you were in a position like I was. The lack of experience really affected the quality of the program.

Q: What were the successes you encountered in building an information security awareness program?

A: My coworkers found a lot of value in my newsletters. I approached security issues that my coworkers face every day at home: phishing (from fake banks), malware, passwords. The idea was if they care about these issues at home, it'll translate to the workplace.

Q: What advice do you have for people who are currently building their own information security awareness programs?

A: Just give it a shot. There are plenty of resources out there. There is a NIST document for security awareness. SANS has great amount of content. Make sure you get continuous feedback and make the program fun. If it's boring, it's ineffective. If your program is ineffective, you're wasting everyone's time.

SECURITY RESEARCH AT LARGE INFORMATION SECURITY COMPANY

This interviewee did not want his name attached to this interview because he works at a company that sells prebuilt information security awareness products.

Q: Thanks for taking part in this Q&A. Please tell us about yourself.

A: In the past life, I was the senior systems engineer for a managed IT services company and the head of security. I included secure architecture into the systems we designed and delivered and provided SAT courses.

Q: What constitutes an information security awareness program in your opinion?

A: It has to start from the top level of the organization. You have to have management and C level buy-in to build and establish a program. At the very basics, a security awareness program teaches the users what to look for and not to be tricked by hackers and persons of malicious intent. Once you have a program and you begin testing it, when you have users who do not fall for phishing campaigns or report attempts at trying to be socially engineered over the phone, you've succeeded. A true program also tests the upper levels of management and C levels to see if they will get through their title in the wind as the reason why they need access to certain data or will break company policy because "it's my company."

Q: What was the reason for building your own program?

A: I established my own program out of need. At the company I worked at previously, we were desperate to have security in our daily lives. I saw the need and I filled it. By the end, everyone was on board, and as a company, we were able to provide much better services to our customers because we could assure them their data were safe with us because of XYZ reason.

Q: How did you get management buy-in for your program?

A: I showed management the need for a program. I did a simple audit of our infrastructure as well as our people and current policies were in place. I showed how easily an attacker could get in and steal our secrets as well as I showed how simple changes would make it that much harder for an attacker. Once I showed it at a low technical level, the program sold itself.

Q: What was your biggest challenge to building an information security awareness program for your organization?

A: Getting people to accept change. Change is hard. No one likes it and everyone seemingly does everything they can to resist it. I went with the approach of let's give this a try for two weeks. If it doesn't work for us, we'll revisit it. At the end of the two-week period, everyone was in sync and the old way was forgotten about.

Q: Was budget an issue?

A: No it was not. I found cost-affordable solutions that could be deployed.

Q: What were the political obstacles that needed to be overcome?

A: The resistance to change as I mentioned above is the biggest obstacle. Also, the thought of testing and the users not being aware they were being tested. No one wants to fail. It had to be made clear it was a test and the outcome would NOT have an impact on performance reviews.

Q: What metrics are useful for measuring the success of an information security awareness program?

A: An internal phishing campaign to users and social engineering attempts and then rating how many fell for it and how many didn't.

Q: What failures and pitfall did you encounter in building an information security awareness program?

A: I would have had failures had I not consulted people of a like mind and sought guidance. Don't assume people know everything. No one knows everything.

Q: What learning and teaching styles did you use for your program?

A: I showed users how quickly as an attacker I could pull an e-mail list out of thin air using services like Maltego and theHarvester. Then how quickly I could clone their Web site and record credentials when they were entered using SET. It scared some people but it made everyone sit up and listen.

Q: What is your advice for others building their own programs?

A: Talk to other people who have done it. Seek advice and ask questions.

Q: What is the advantage of building your own program over buying a prebuilt information security awareness program from a vendor?

A: Because prebuilt isn't made for your company. They're not tailored and will not cover everything that you need to be successful.

Q: What were the successes you encountered in building an information security awareness program?

A: The successes came when users started to correctly identify malicious attempts by attackers. Instead of clicking on a link, they would report it and move on. That felt great.

Q: What advice do you have for people who are currently building their own information security awareness programs?

A: Don't quit. It takes a lot of effort but it's worth it.

HARRY REGAN

Mr. Harry Regan, CISSP, CISM, is a security, information technology, and operations professional with over 30 years of commercial, federal, and defense experience. He has functioned in executive, senior technical staff, and consulting engagements with assignments encompassing corporate and program management, computer and network operations, and executive-level consulting. Mr. Regan has extensive experience with physical security, as well as information security and privacy program development, threat and vulnerability assessments, technology countermeasures, supervisory control and data acquisition (SCADA) systems, building and industrial infrastructure protection, NERC critical infrastructure protection (NERC CIP), and regulatory compliance. Mr.

Regan received a BA in Economics from Catholic University and an MS in Information Technology and Operations Research from the American University.

Q: Thanks for taking part in this Q&A. Please tell us about yourself.

A: Between 2002 and 2008, I ran a small security consultancy focused on financial services, healthcare, and higher-education security issues. In 2004 and 2005, I was engaged to collaborate on a series of security awareness training modules for a state college system. There were three tiers of training—student, faculty/staff, and management.

Q: What constitutes an information security awareness program in your opinion?

A: A security awareness program needs to educate the attendees as to why they should be trained, provide guidance as to activities and behaviors that are dangerous, explain why those activities are dangerous, and provide examples of the ramifications of what noncompliance is— that is, personal or institutional harm, penalties, and liability.

Q: What was the reason for building your own program?

A: As with many college systems, the state had suffered a number of data breaches and was facing penalties under the Gramm–Leach–Bliley (GLBA) Act and other privacy legislation. The lack of adequate data protection and end-user education has reached the state Attorney General's attention and a mandate to rectify the security programs in all state agencies was issued.

Q: How did you get management buy-in for your program?

A: In this case, it was easy—threats of loss of autonomy from the agency from the Attorney General's Office were the biggest business driver.

Q: What was your biggest challenge to building an information security awareness program for your organization?

A: Our biggest challenge was the balance of freedom versus openness. In academic environments, free expression of ideas, sharing of information, and openness in discussing conflicting ideas are emphasized. But the concept of a security program in general with rules and restrictions and controls runs against the grain with many of the stakeholders. The very idea of a formal security program—even though specifically called for under GLBA—was a point for rigorous debate, rather than being accepted as an operational necessity.

Q: Was budget an issue?

A: Yes. The Attorney General's Office took the position that the college system should have already had a mature security program in place already—including a security awareness program—so this was an "unfunded mandate."

Q: What where the political obstacles that needed to be overcome?

A: When we started building the program, we had to debate the legal team on whether we could or could not say something was a regulatory violation. We were constantly being accused of helping the Security Manager in empire building. The best weapon we had against that was periodic letters from the Attorney General's Office threatening to put state auditors in the system to oversee operations.

Q: What metrics are useful for measuring the success of an information security awareness program?

A: Using a learning management system as the training delivery mechanism and having quizzes embedded in the material allowed us to track both the completion metrics and the embedded training metrics—so over time, you could see improvements in understanding not only during the training but also at the end of training.

Q: What failures and pitfall did you encounter in building an information security awareness program?

A: The student version was successfully implemented. The staff and management training got mired in pushback and political turmoil, the reasoning being phrased as a resource and priority problem: we don't have time to take this training—besides we are professionals and don't need this training, so it's a low priority that I take it—continued malware outbreaks and network breaches notwithstanding.

Q: What is the best training cycle for a program?

A: In my opinion, semiyearly is the best cycle. I believe that more frequent than that makes the program a chore to be dealt with rather than a beneficial refresher. But I also believe that the program needs to be revised and refreshed on a semiyearly cycle as well, so that people are not seeing the exact same material over and over. In programs like that, people just tune out at some point.

Q: What learning and teaching styles did you use for your program?

A: We used a situational approach:

- Separate training by role—students, faculty/staff, and management received different trainings.
- Story narrative—we used a series of vignettes with different characters demonstrating good and bad security behavior to punctuate points in the training.
- Embedded quizzes—were used to test knowledge at points during the training and capturing the quiz results in addition to the final results.

Q: What is your advice for others building their own programs?

A: Don't plan security awareness and a once-and-done program. It has to be reviewed and renewed as technologies and threats change. It has to be germane to the audience as well—not a one-size-fits-all approach. Lastly, and probably the most difficult to achieve, it has to be engaging to the audience—having a series of slides simply preaching to the user is an approach that will fail.

Q: What is the advantage of building your own program over buying a prebuilt information security awareness program from a vendor?

A: Building your own allows a degree of customization most prebuilt programs can't touch. Also, if you build your program using a learning management platform (Moodle, DigitalChalk, etc.), you can use that same platform for other training and collaborative sessions as well.

Q: What where the successes you encountered in building an information security awareness program?

A: We had our best success with the student version and our worst time with the management version. The management tier seemed to be saying "Security education is important for my team—but I can't afford to take the time...."

Q: What advice do you have for people who are currently building their own information security awareness programs?

A: Don't assume your audience has *any* technical background. Even terms like Web, URL, and network may require some context for some users. Be conscious of your tone in the training—don't preach—don't dictate. Rather, inform and try to bring your audience along with you—this is much easier to say than to do. It is perfectly okay if the users are entertained while they are learning!

Q: Is there anything we haven't covered that you would like to add?

A: Remember, what you're putting together is a "system," so you should go through requirements, design, development, and test phases. Have real users test the content and flow before general release is always a good idea—and be willing to accept criticism.

TESS SCHRODINGER

Tess Schrodinger has twenty years in law enforcement, investigation, forensics (bullets and blood, not 1 s and 0 s), and industrial security. She holds a bachelors degree in sociology from George Mason University, a master's degree in security management, and a graduate certificate in Cyber Security Technology.

Q: Thanks for taking part in this Q&A. Please tell us about yourself.

A: Thanks for asking me to contribute!

When I was a little girl, there was a book I read about a girl who collected ways to defeat different dangerous situations that was similar to the popular The Worst-Case Scenario Survival Handbook that was published many years later. There was something about learning all these interesting tips and tricks and methods to defeat situations that threatened your life or security, and all these years later, I still enjoy learning about new threats and then ways to mitigate or neutralize them. So, to me, it is just as interesting to learn how to escape quicksand as it is to secure my laptop. And, I like to share what I have learned with others.

I have approximately 15 + years in forensics and security. I am one of those people that if I won the lottery, I would probably retire and "go to school" for forever (taking long breaks off to explore the world). I love to learn and I love to teach and share. I homeschool my daughter with the help of my retired parents and I have been a proponent of education and security awareness for almost my entire life.

Q: What constitutes an information security awareness program in your opinion?

A: In my opinion, an information security awareness program is truly robust if it is planned, is consistent, and targets a specific audience.

"Planned" means that is not an occasional occurrence or an afterthought. A planned program will have a clearly stated objective, a defined focus, and a specific audience or set of audiences. Planned also means it's not a lethargic half-assed response to a mandatory contractual requirement that is so minimal that it barely meets the expectations at best or is just "going through the motions."

"Consistent" means that it's not a one-time occurrence like an initial security brief that is long forgotten years later. There is repetition of material and testing of the staff to see if they are retaining or getting value from the program and then adjusting the approach accordingly to accommodate your assessment of the impact. I attended a course in how to create a security awareness program and one of the things that was echoed was that you have to tell someone something ten times for them to maybe register it once. I have always taken that advice to heart, so I don't just cover a topic once, I cover it multiple times but I keep it fresh by reiterating the same message but changing up the method of presentation.

A "specific audience" means that the materials and presentations are tailored to the audience. Thought is given to ensuring that their level of education, background, and current responsibilities are taken into account when the material is presented to them. "One size fits all" is better than nothing but it is not the optimal approach. When I sit down with my team composed of programmers and network specialists, I do not use the same presentation that I would with a group of administrative assistants. I may be conveying the same message but I need to speak in their language to their level and put the material in a context that makes it relevant to them so they do not tune me out.

Q: What was the reason for building your own program?

A: There is a contractual requirement in my world to provide a minimum level of security awareness and education. I would have done it anyway but I confess I have used the "mandated" aspect of things to "motivate" a few surly antieducation types to attend.

Q: How did you get management buy-in for your program?

A: My management understands the contractual requirement for a program and is relatively supportive to the program, but there have definitely been budgetary issues in the few recent years that have affected the program.

What I have found over the years is that when you speak to leadership or management, you are often speaking to people who are not focused on security so much as they are focused on dollars. I think it is imperative to be able to translate the risk of neglecting to educate your users into a dollar amount and learn how to illustrate a solid return on investment (ROI) to them.

I once worked very closely with the general counsel of a firm. He was a very busy man and a very intelligent man, but most of the time, he did not see the value of educating our people. He was not against it but he was also not seeing that it was worth the effort. One day, I sat down with him and I laid a pair of handcuffs on the table. He looked at them with raised eyebrows and I explained that if we did what I was suggesting, there was a good chance he would not be on CNN wearing those any time soon. Suddenly that synapse fired and he saw the value. For him, it was not dollars that did it but a possible legal charge or arrest if he was negligent.

Management is going to come from different backgrounds and is sometimes motivated by different agendas, but I found that if you can communicate to them the value of educating the staff, they will get the message and they will support you. For years after that handcuff incident, my general counsel would introduce me to folks as "the woman that keeps me out of jail!"

Learn how the business mind thinks. Learn how to translate the value of educating staff into a language they will understand, not just when educating them but when soliciting buy-in from leadership to support and fund your security awareness efforts.

Q: What was your biggest challenge to building an information security awareness program for your organization?

A: I have a wide range of staff I have to educate. They range from janitorial staff to highly technical engineer types. I learned early on that I had to tailor my approach. Getting the basics across to an on-site vendor that barely speaks English is going to be different than delivering the same message to a very busy engineer who already feels like they know everything and can't be bothered to waste time listening to what I have to say.

I have also found that security can be especially dry and boring to many who don't live in our world. Users often fail to see how they can be targeted and they are often ignorant as to the threats that are around them or the vulnerabilities they can pose through their own actions. Security is also often inconvenient or out of their normal pattern of behavior so it's a change they are being asked to make that can be mentally or physically uncomfortable to many. Couple that with the incredible speed at which new threats and attack vectors occur, it's enough to make some people throw up their hands and give up. When it comes to technology-related security, I have heard many people state that they just can't keep up and don't have the slightest idea of how to even begin to start or keep up once they have so they decide to just do nothing.

Q: Was budget an issue?

A: I am fortunate enough to have a small budget but it has definitely been slashed, and to be honest, I often supplement with my own money because I feel it is important and I have seen enough of a return on investment that I don't feel bad about contributing. I will often purchase treats or pick up a little prize to give away to those who attend my briefings. I got a Starbucks' card or last year I got those little mini books with the Spy versus Spy figurines for $8 and gave one of those away at each of my monthly briefings. I once calculated that it's worth the $8 to me personally to not have to stay overnight or on a weekend to clean up a mess they've made because they didn't know any better.

Q: What were the political obstacles that needed to be overcome?

A: Dealing with the group that handles all of the organization's communications has been the most frustrating. I have had occasions where I have put together an entire series of e-mail messages to be used for a year for my team and I have had that group come back and have me change the shade of green in the banner. While I do understand some of the changes that need to be made from a 508 compliance perspective (something I have learned a lot about recently), many of the changes they demand have no rhyme or reason to them and it can be incredibly frustrating to continuously have to rework education materials with numerous small changes over and over again.

Many years ago, I proposed an active shooter briefing that I was forbidden to do because "it might be scary" to the staff. I rather thought it would be a heck of a lot scarier to be trapped in our facility with an active shooter and not know what to do but they ignored me. It gets frustrating sometimes when a group of people that have nothing to do with security and know absolutely nothing about security suddenly decide they want to tinker with your content or forbid it outright. But, I have learned ways to be flexible and ways to get my message across that do not involve formal approval by a group of red pencil-wielding people who have nothing better to do than to nitpick my font choice and color selections or try to sanitize everything to the point where it can't possibly offend anyone. There are times when I do have to deal with them and get formal approvals so I try to work within what I have learned their parameters are but I do my best to avoid it if at all possible.

Q: What metrics are useful for measuring the success of an information security awareness program?

A: In my opinion, employee reporting is one of the biggest metrics I use to measure the success of my program. When I first took over my sites, there was pretty much no reporting of any types of suspicious behavior or questions around security concerns. Several years later, I can hold up binders full of reports from my staff of suspicious behavior reporting and personal reporting and several binders of suspicious e-mails forwarded to me.

I think the moment I realized I was making an impact and people were listening was when the head of our IT department had sent out an e-mail to the entire organization to do something and almost 100% of my staff refused to do it until I confirmed that his e-mail was legitimate and it was not a "trick." I had just one week before that I told them about how it was possible for people to hack the e-mail accounts of a senior leader or send e-mails that look like they come from important internal departments. I actually had a project manager tell his entire team to hold until he had cleared it with me. While this was incredibly annoying to have to deal with several hundred frantics and worried phone calls and e-mails over the next 24 h, it was also pretty awesome to see how many people had paid attention and forwarded his e-mail to me with words to the effect of, "I remember that stuff you told us and I am not going to do this unless YOU say it's okay!"

Another time, I had sent an e-mail to one of my staff requesting some information I needed. I had just recently done a briefing on social engineering and part of me wondered if they would even question it but so often you feel like no one is listening to you so I didn't think much of it. I had to smile when they replied with a "test" saying they'd be happy to get that information to me but they wanted to make sure I was who I said I was so would I please tell them my son's name. I don't have a son, I have a daughter so I smiled and replied to them with the correct information and ALSO corrected another comment they had made about my boyfriend who was overseas at the time as they knew where he was but had deliberately asked how he was enjoying his stay in a completely different country. They apologized for "questioning" me, as many senior leadership types often get angry if challenged or questioned but I praised the fact they paid attention and stopped to question my request. I have had many more instances like this and I feel that reporting metric is what truly shows how effective my program has been.

Q: What failures and pitfalls did you encounter in building an information security awareness program?

A: After knocking the wood of the desk I am sitting at, I can say with pride that I have not really had any failures in building my programs. I did almost have a hurricane take out one of my events one year but we managed to skirt it. Pitfalls, again, would be dealing with people who feel they should have some role in approving my material when they don't understand it and seem determined to justify their own jobs by insisting on a series of edits or changes or feel that the material is too scary or potentially offensive to present to staff. By potentially offensive, I am referring to their constant need to sanitize every aspect of an item. I once, and I am not kidding, reformatted an entire series of e-mail communications to accommodate their request that they all be in Arial instead of Times New Roman. I made all the changes (due to the formatting, it wasn't a quick highlight and change) and thought I was done. It took them two and a half weeks to come back and insist I change the Arial font from 11 point to 10 point. That's when I had to take one of my infamous "time-outs" and go to Starbucks so I wouldn't make inappropriate comments in a work environment.

Q: What is the best training cycle for a program?

A: My personal training cycle consists of the following:

1. An initial security briefing before they start work. This is usually done during the first week but sometimes I will be flexible and coordinate with them to accommodate special projects they are on. I have briefed staff in hotel lobbies, cars, bars, and other places. I keep a copy of my initial briefing (it does not contain any sensitive or proprietary data) on my iPad and I make sure I work closely with my project managers to ensure everyone gets briefed in a timely manner and their first brief is in-depth and thorough.
2. A monthly theme that I put out a small presentation on. Most of my folks are incredibly busy and do not have much spare time to read or review volumes of material. I will use custom-made graphics as e-mail signatures that link to my internal network site where they can look at current and past materials. I will e-mail the presentation to those who are off-site or

working in a remote location. Once a year, I will have a security refresher briefing for all staff to remind them of their responsibilities, update them on any new threats or vectors of concern, and educate them on any new regulations or requirements they need to be aware of or that are coming down the pike.

3. A yearly theme/topic that I usually gear a series of monthly brown bags around. If you only offer one briefing on a topic once a year, then you only get the people that can make that one briefing. Instead, I will select a Friday each month and offer a brief at lunch time that people can attend. This way, instead of them only having one opportunity a year to make the briefing, they will have twelve opportunities.

4. A yearly one-time large security awareness day event. I will typically bring in several speakers and arrange to serve lunch. I try to make sure the presenters are entertaining and interesting and on subjects that will be of interest. There exists a wealth of resources who would be happy to come in and speak to your people; all you have to do is ask.

5. Special one-off briefings that address specific current concerns or threats that have evolved or presented themselves.

Q: What learning and teaching styles did you use for your program?

A: I try to keep my security education fun and interesting. I have movie posters from various genres having to do with security hanging in my office. Decoration? Sure. But they also prompt conversation. If you get someone talking about something that interests them, you can often slide security into the discussion in a relevant way that has context and then it's interesting and they are really listening because they are talking about something they enjoy not struggling to stay awake while you drone on in front of a conference room. I can slip security into a conversation on anything from Star Trek to James Bond to Doctor Who.

I also keep books and different cartoons in my office to try and make those anchor connections with people. They can't help but scan my bookshelf when they come in, and usually, there is a title that catches their eye and prompts a question or suggestion from them. I have over 400 people I am responsible for educating and I know who my runners are, I know who my foodies are, and I know which ones are Trekkies and which prefer Star Wars. I know who my former military officers are and my LEOs (law enforcement officers). As I learn more about my staff or their likes and dislikes, I try to tailor my training to them. An example would be the recent March Madness. No offense, but I am not at all into basketball. My office, however, was very excited about it. I came up with the idea of March Security Madness and did an entire basketball theme around it to include a suspicious behavior reporting bracket for them to hang in their cubes.

Posters are a great tool and I use those around my different facilities, making sure to change them out periodically so they don't get boring. There are a number of free poster sources online and you can also browse a Google image search of "security education posters" and make your own using ideas you find there. I'll often see a poster idea and then customize it to work for my site or topic.

Many of my folks are super busy so I try to keep my education short and sweet other than the initial brief when I have them hostage for an hour or during my annual awareness event when I can fit in a few blocks of longer briefings or presentations.

I try to keep things "sexy." Humor goes a long way but try and keep it in good taste so you don't end up having issues with HR for offending people. I find puns and things that are relatively safe for the elementary school-age level are usually pretty safe for the work place.

I try to be respectful during religious holidays by going with a seasonal theme such as "winter" or "spring" and staying away from "Christmas" or "Easter." Big bright catchy colors go a long way and cartoons and visuals can often convey an entire page of bullet points in a much more entertaining way. Think of things that go hand in hand with that season. For example, I once did a TRASHINT piece around the Christmas holidays and pointed out what nosy folks could learn about them from the boxes they threw away after presents were opened. I had actually prepared for that the year before by taking photos in my neighborhood of people's trash at the curb and then posting photos and asking, "Which house would YOU rob?" or "Who has which laptop or router or game system?"

I keep a large bulletin board in each facility that is devoted to security awareness education. I will sit down each New Year and pick twelve topics I want to cover that year and figure out a theme to tie to each. I will create an e-mail signature that ties into that topic and then post a print out of a small short deck I created on the bulletin board. It's usually only nice slides because that's what I can fit on my board, three across and three down. Sometimes, I will go by the party store and get rolls of wrapping paper or those inexpensive cardboard cutouts to spiff the board up or catch everyone's attention. If you are thinking to yourself that this sounds suspiciously like those bulletin boards they had in each classroom in elementary school, you would be CORRECT! That is, the idea only geared toward a more adult audience!

Once I have posted the boards, I will then upload the PowerPoint presentation to my internal security site on our firm's intranet and link the signature picture in my e-mail to it. This way, the folks I have that work remotely or on-site in distant states still get exposed to the material.

Once each year, I will host a security awareness day and I will bring in speakers and internal vendors to talk to my staff. It can be difficult to command an audience at a voluntary event like that but I have found providing food whether it's popcorn or cupcakes or when I get the occasional approval for budget I will provide lunch. I try to bring in those I have heard speak before and who have an interesting message. It doesn't always even have to do specifically with security, but if I know my folks are really interested in something, I will try to bring someone in for that topic. One year, I managed to arrange to bring in a polygraph examiner from a local agency and he spent almost two hours explaining the process and equipment in detail and then hooked various people up and taught the entire audience how to read the results along with him. It was an absolutely standing room only but many people came to the briefing prior to that or staid for the one after that so it was not necessarily a topic I needed to provide education on but one I knew they would be interested in.

I also make an effort to invite other security professionals to my big event. I will go through the building to each business and speak to their security person or department and then invite them to come. When they are there, I make sure to introduce them to the contacts I have and help them form new relationships to strengthen their security programs as well.

Many federal and local agencies have public or business liaisons that will come speak for free as it's part of their job to reach out and do things like that. I am a certified antiterrorism officer levels I and II and can brief on that topic, but to all my staff, I'm just "Tess" and it's not very exciting. BUT if I bring in a man with a gun and a badge who is from somewhere else, suddenly, it's like I have brought in a rock star to dazzle them with exciting information and stories! We could present the exact same material but it's different when I bring in a stranger to do it. I take advantage of that and use it to build excitement in the staff to attend the talk.

Q: What is your advice for others building their own programs?

A: Marketing. You have to market yourself and your program not only to the staff you are trying to educate but also to the leadership you are trying to get support and money from. Take some time to learn how marketers use colors or themes or ideas to capture attention and communicate messages. Don't expect your people to read something just because you told them to. Make them WANT to read it.

Be creative and interesting. Think about how you like to learn. Would you rather have me drone on and on and on about why it's important we wear our badges and report unescorted strangers or would you rather have me post a few posters and then reward those who "capture" unbadged strangers in our space and turn them in with gift cards to Starbucks or giant candy bars? (Yes, I have done both of these.)

Be approachable. I have found over the years that many people in security treat users like idiots and they can feel that vibe either consciously or subconsciously. Being someone they can talk to means they will also be more likely to listen to you. Remember that this is not their job and they are not educated like you. It may seem like a total no brainer to you to lock your computer when you get up to use the restroom but put yourself in the shoes of an older administrative assistant who is still a bit overwhelmed by Facebook (like my mom) and something that simple doesn't even occur to them. Many people are pretty decent folks at heart and don't think like an adversary or bad guy so it's just foreign to them to think someone will steal from them or use their systems to do bad things. There is no need to terrify them into submission but this is something you have to keep in mind as you are educating them on how to keep themselves and the enterprise safe. Don't just tell them what to do, tell them WHY to do it and what could happen if they don't. Then, reinforce that with stories and case studies to make it REAL to them and not just "stuff that happens in those James Bond picture shows."

Reward them! Yes. Reward them. When they do good, give them a pat on the back. HAVE their back when necessary. I recently had a young woman who was very new to my organization challenge an old grizzled senior that tried to piggyback into the facility with her when he forgot his badge one day. He yelled at her for questioning who he was and really gave her a hard time. Her boss asked me to say something and I did. I made sure to send an e-mail out to the entire site praising her questioning a stranger trying to access our site and that she had done the right thing. I then had a talk with the man who yelled at her and he ended up apologizing to her for his behavior.

Another time, I had a receptionist come to me with a concern around someone trying to access one of my server rooms. To begin with, I was rather stunned she even registered that this was odd but to tie it to the fact it was the server room really amazed me. I checked it out and it was indeed... something to be interested in. I was so proud of her that I sent out an e-mail to the entire team and her boss and praised her for catching what she did. I asked some of the senior leadership to personally stop by her desk and thank her and make an appreciative comment to her and I also nominated her for a small internal award. She told me later that I made her feel like a super star but that it also reinforced her desire to want to do a good job and do what was good for the team. Adults, like children, often react better to positive reinforcement than negative punishment so I encourage you to recognize your folks, whether it's an e-mail to the team, a formal letter to their boss, nominating them for an award, or just simply going to their office and saying, "Thank YOU."

Q: What is the advantage of building your own program over buying a prebuilt information security awareness program from a vendor?

A: This is a hard question for me to answer because I have never purchased a prebuilt security awareness program from a vendor so I really can't make that sort of comparison. Instead, I will say that the reasons I do NOT purchase a security awareness program from a vendor are as follows:

1. Cost. I don't mind buying a $20 Starbucks card to give away to one lucky user who comes to my briefing but I don't have the budget to purchase a formal prebuilt education product and I am not going to pay out of my own pocket.
2. It's a one-size-fits-all solution that I'd have to tailor anyway OR pay extra to have tailored.
3. You are stuck with what they give you and if you don't like it, that's it.
4. I have skills and resources to create my own for virtually no cost.

If the decision is between buying a prebuilt product and not having any security education at all, by all means, BUY IT! But if you have the skills and some creativity and enjoy teaching others, I don't see any distinct disadvantage of doing it yourself.

Q: What were the successes you encountered in building an information security awareness program?

A: My biggest successes have been seeing a tremendous increase in people coming to me with concerns, questions, or requesting guidance.

Q: What advice do you have for people who are currently building their own information security awareness programs?

A: Respect your audience. Understand what they do and do not know and solicit their feedback. Don't speak down to them or be condescending. Try to keep things short enough to respect their time yet comprehensive enough to get the message across. Keep in mind that while this is your job to educate them, they might not recognize that it is also their job to learn from you. I find that if you make things fun or interesting, it engages them more and makes them want to listen and make that connection. Don't make security another chore, make it something they want to do or, at the very least, don't "hate" to do. Obviously, you will always have that one person that hates everything but I have found this works pretty well in general.

Q: Is there anything we haven't covered that you would like to add?

A: Something that is very big in my world is sharing. Some of us are good at coming up with ideas or materials and others truly struggle with it. One of the things I have noted is that so many folks in this community are more than happy to share their materials with you. If you are one of those that is good at it, then I encourage you to share if you are able to. While I have respect for those who are trying to make a living off of selling security awareness materials, not every security program has the luxury of that kind of cost. And some programs don't even have budgets at all. Reach out to the security community and you will find they are usually fairly happy to share resources and materials with you.

SECURITY ANALYST AT A NETWORK SECURITY COMPANY

This interviewee wished to remain anonymous due to his work in the defense industry.

Q: What constitutes an information security awareness program in your opinion?

A: An InfoSec awareness program is all encompassing of an organization's information. It covers much more than just computer security. It covers how employees deal with the information that they have in their brain about the organization and information they provide or is given to them about the organization in the course of their normal duties within the organization. This covers not only anything from computers to telephones but also such mundane things as discussing an organization's information in a public place such as a restaurant.

Q: What was the reason for building your own program?

A: In the course of my employment within different Department of Defense (DOD) organizations such as the Department of Defense Dependents Schools (DoDDS), Defense Logistics Agency (DLA), or US Army, information security awareness was an ongoing effort. While DOD has an overall awareness program, it is always best to customize and target different types of personnel with different levels of awareness. The awareness that a system administrator, an executive assistance to the General Officer, a school principal, or a K–12 teacher need to have is vastly different.

Within DOD, there are also operations security (OPSEC) and counterintelligence (CI) awareness programs. In many aspects, these programs overlap because obtaining information that employees know or have access too is what the opposition is attempting to obtain.

Q: How did you get management buy-in for your program?

A: Since it was a mandated training for all of DOD, there was no need to get buy-in from management. The most difficult part was tracking the percentage of employees who had fulfilled their annual requirement for training. Even with an automated system to track these numbers, the percentages fluctuated with employees been hired, retiring, or leaving the organization to work elsewhere. It was hard to get management to accept that these numbers would fluctuate and that achieving 100% on a large organization that is always in flux was not going to happen on a certain date.

Q: What was your biggest challenge to building an information security awareness program for your organization?

A: To convey to employees that this training was necessary and tracking the percentage of employees who had taken their training for management reporting. It took a long time for people to understand the necessity of such training, but as real-world examples could be shown, people understood the requirement for the training.

Q: Was budget an issue?

A: No, budget was not an issue due to the mandate for the training applied to all of DOD.

Q: What where the political obstacles that needed to be overcome?

A: The biggest political obstacle was the syndrome of "another annual training requirement" that was expressed by both employees and management.

Q: What metrics are useful for measuring the success of an information security awareness program?

A: The number of employees who had completed their training requirement. Ongoing random testing by an organization is also very useful, having a team perform phishing, telephone-based social engineering, or attempted physical access tests whether employees have absorbed and are actually applying the information that is conveyed during the training. Success is tracking these metrics over several years and showing an improving trend. As with auto accidents, they will happen, the goal is to have an ongoing downward trend.

Q: What failures and pitfall did you encounter in building an information security awareness program?

A: Even though employees received awareness training about phishing, many still fell victim to them and gave up log-in credentials. I believe that awareness training is something that you must do and that not having a security awareness program so makes the situation worse by admitting defeat. Looking at this from another perspective, what if the program prevents several attempts targeted as personnel that could have resulted in *large or catastrophic compromise of* information? You may never find out about that success since the program was effective in that instance.

Q: What is the best training cycle for a program?

A: The training is required on an annual basis. Since DOD employees must also take training that overlaps with similar topics and content, the training was required to be done within 1 year. This was automatically scheduled within the online learning management system. Employees were notified via e-mail when the training was due. Some employees took the training right away once they were notified that it was added to their learning plan; others waited until they received their 30-day notice. Once an employee took the training, it was automatically scheduled again with a due date 1 year from the last completion date.

Q: What learning and teaching styles did you use for your program?

A: Due to the volume of employees, the training was provided via computer-based training. The training materials changed each year and were uniform across all of DOD. Other portions of the security awareness program are always performed via an in-person instructor-led sessions, such as the CI awareness training.

Q: What is your advice for others building their own programs?

A: Be creative! The program needs to go beyond just another annual training requirement. This includes everything from awareness posters hanging in common areas to coffee shop $5 gift cards for answering a question during an instructor-led training session. You are essentially marketing or selling this information to the intended audience; if you can't gain their attention, you won't accomplish much.

Q: What is the advantage of building your own program over buying a prebuilt information security awareness program from a vendor?

A: Customization! While you can supplement a prebuilt program with additional materials, the information may not be exactly what your organization needs if using a prebuilt program. It may be best to start out with a prebuilt program to get your awareness program off the ground and then tailor it specifically to your organization by doing your own organic materials in the future.

Q: What where the successes you encountered in building an information security awareness program?

A: After people experience that the awareness training can apply both to their personal information and to the organization's information, they see the positive aspect of having to the take the training. One employee commented to me that a stranger approached him to borrow his BlackBerry to make a phone call while waiting at a bus stop. The employee declined because something didn't feel right and that was confirmed when the stranger pulled out his own phone to make a call several minutes later.

The greatest success I experienced was making a video about the threat that 802.11 wireless presents to organizations. This was while I was part of the Regional Computer Emergency Response Team (RCERT)–Europe in

Mannheim, Germany. We made the video using a van parked in a Walmart parking lot with a large antenna aimed several hundred feet away at an office building just inside the perimeter fence of the Army installation. The video showed us wardriving at first, detecting the access point, and then parking to exploit a server via the wireless network.

The video was memorable and stuck in people's heads because in addition to the humans, we placed 4 ft inflatable aliens within the video. One rode shotgun in the passenger seat of the van, one stood by the antenna in the parking lot, and other looked on as the server was exploited. While this video was intended to US Army personnel in Europe, it made the rounds all over Army installations worldwide. It was even adopted by the Army Signal School at Fort Gordon. Even though the video was totally staged and no Army network was ever in any danger, the association of the aliens with the danger of wireless stuck in people's minds. The video was made in 2002, and years later, people still asked about the video once they knew I worked at the RCERT–Europe. Plus, now it is in this survey too!

Q: What advice do you have for people who are currently building their own information security awareness programs?

A: Be creative! The program needs to go beyond just another annual training requirement. You are essentially marketing or selling this program to the intended audience; if you can't gain their attention, you won't accomplish much. If your organization has a sales department, use the talent within that department to come up with a marketing strategy. If you have a public relations personnel, ask them for advice to how to best reach your audience. Remember that many people won't remember much of the Super Bowl game each year other than a few highlights of the game and those 30 s commercials—your program needs to have few key nuggets of InfoSec that people will remember!

Q: Is there anything we haven't covered that you would like to add?

A: Nope.

ERNIE HAYDEN

Ernie is a highly experienced and seasoned technical consultant, author, speaker, strategist, and thought leader with extensive experience in the power utility industry, critical infrastructure protection/information security domain, industrial control system, cybercrime, and cyberwarfare areas. His primary emphasis is on project and business development involving cyber and physical security of industrial controls, smart grid, energy supply, and oil/gas/electric systems and facilities with special expertise on industrial controls and NERC critical infrastructure protection (NERC CIP) standards. Hayden has held roles as Global Managing Principal–Critical Infrastructure/Industrial Controls Security at Verizon, held information security officer/manager positions at the Port of Seattle, Group Health Cooperative (Seattle), ALSTOM ESCA and Seattle City Light. In 2012, Ernie was named a "Smart Grid Pioneer" by SmartGridToday and published an article on Microgrid security in Jesse Berst's SmartGridNews. Ernie is a frequent author of blogs, opinion pieces, and white papers. He has been cited in the Financial Times, Boston Globe, EnergyBiz Magazine, and Puget Sound Business Journal. Many of his articles have been posted to such forums as Energy Central, Public Utilities Fortnightly "SPARK," and his own blog on infrastructure security. He is an invited columnist for the "Ask the Experts" discussions on www.searchsecurity.com and he published an article regarding electric grid security versus compliance in Public Utilities Fortnightly magazine. Other thought-leadership articles have included a chapter on "Cybercrime's Impact on Information Security," in the Oxford University Press Cybercrime and Security Legal Series, and several articles in Information Security Magazine, including his original research on data life cycle security and an article on data breaches in the same publication. Ernie is a very active contributor in global security forums. His past includes membership in the Cloud Security Alliance where he was the leader for the Information Lifecycle Domain in the Cloud Security Guidelines document Version 2. He has also been an instructor, curriculum developer, and advisor for the University of Washington Information System Security Certificate program in Seattle.

Q: What constitutes an information security awareness program in your opinion?

A: The key point for an information security awareness program is to get the regular employee to be your first line of defense for the information security program. In other words, they need to be aware that their actions (or inactions) can lead to breaches of data and the security of the company. Hence, they need to understand that their role is the everyday eyes and ears for the company's security.

Q: What was the reason for building your own program?

A: I have held the equivalent of four CISO positions—each one was the first true information security manager for each of the companies. Hence, the security program I needed to enact was truly a start-up for each company. One area that I included in each of the companies was a security awareness program of one sort or another.

My reason for this was as noted above—I view each employee to be the first line of the company's defense for InfoSec. Hence, they need to understand their roles and they need to understand what to do if they see a problem that could be indicative of an InfoSec issue in progress.

Q: How did you get management buy-in for your program?

A: The management buy-in was relatively easy since the management wanted a security awareness program anyway. The management caused some challenges when they were concerned that InfoSec became a "police function," and then in one company, the management was very strong in stopping the program until it was modified (e.g., putting notes on chairs if an unattended desktop was unlocked was viewed as being too much a "police function" and needed to stop).

Q: What was your biggest challenge to building an information security awareness program for your organization?

A: The biggest challenge is time: the time it took to develop the program, the time it took to develop the presentations, etc. That was the biggest issue since all four security awareness programs were built along the concept of "guerilla marketing"—basically quick, cheap, and effective. This detracted from me doing my other roles.

Q: Was budget an issue?

A: Budget was an issue—there were no funds for a "formal" security awareness program. But I could get some funds for small things like simple handouts and posters, designed and made by me. But, purchasing any security awareness products on the outside was not allowed for the programs due to the lack of funds.

Q: What where the political obstacles that needed to be overcome?

A: The first one at one company was the management's view that InfoSec was and could be a "police function" and they were very worried that security awareness could go too far in this direction.

Otherwise, there weren't too many political obstacles—especially because I made the security awareness program interesting, informative, and fun.

Q: What metrics are useful for measuring the success of an information security awareness program?

A: None—I didn't have time to be that sophisticated. However, I did track how many individuals attended my lunch-and-learn presentations.

Q: What failures and pitfall did you encounter in building an information security awareness program?

A: No failures per se. . . especially since anything being done was more than had ever been done before.

Q: What is the best training cycle for a program?

A: I tried to do presentations for all new employees and monthly.

Q: What learning and teaching styles did you use for your program?

A: One aspect I tried to use was to help the employee best understand how they can protect their own data.

For instance, I would do lunch-and-learn classes in November/early December to teach employees about online/Internet fraud, theft, etc. I would help them best understand good practices for protecting their own passwords, credit card numbers, etc., with the hope and "plan" so to speak that they would bring these good security practices back into the office space.

Q: What is your advice for others building their own programs?

A: Start small, start simple, and every little bit you do "counts." You don't need to buy outside posters, handouts, trinkets, etc., to be successful.

Take advantage of company newsletters. I usually have an article in each newsletter about InfoSec, what to watch out for, etc.

Take advantage of company meetings, new employee orientation for security awareness presentations, etc.

Q: What is the advantage of building your own program over buying a prebuilt information security awareness program from a vendor?

A: I've never used a prebuilt program but my opinion is that your own program can weave in corporate culture, corporate stories, organizational issues, etc., more so than a prebuilt program.

Q: What where the successes you encountered in building an information security awareness program?

A: The occasional person who would thank me for either teaching them how to be more secure or hearing a story about how someone would share a story of a new lesson-learned or how a security near-miss was prevented.

Q: What advice do you have for people who are currently building their own information security awareness programs?

A: Start small, start simple, and every little bit you do "counts." You don't need to buy outside posters, handouts, trinkets, etc., to be successful.

Take advantage of company newsletters. I usually have an article in each newsletter about InfoSec, what to watch out for, etc.

Take advantage of company meetings, new employee orientation for security awareness presentations, etc.

Q: Is there anything we haven't covered that you would like to add?

A: Nope. . . thanks!

Appendices

Bill Gardner
Marshall University, Huntington, WV, USA

APPENDIX A: GOVERNMENT RESOURCES

NIST Special Publication 800-16

http://csrc.nist.gov/publications/nistpubs/800-16/800-16.pdf

NIST Special Publication 800-16 Appendix A-D

http://csrc.nist.gov/publications/nistpubs/800-16/AppendixA-D.pdf

NIST Special Publication 800-16 Appendix E

http://csrc.nist.gov/publications/nistpubs/800-16/Appendix_E.pdf

Statement of Work Computer Security Awareness and Training: April 2000

http://csrc.nist.gov/groups/SMA/fasp/documents/security_ate/SOW-exe.doc

NIST Special Publication 800-50: Building an Information Technology Security Awareness and Training Program

http://csrc.nist.gov/publications/nistpubs/800-50/NIST-SP800-50.pdf

US Department of Health and Human Services: Security Awareness and Training

http://www.hhs.gov/ocio/securityprivacy/awarenesstraining/awarenesstraining.html

National Initiative For Cybersecurity Careers and Studies

http://niccs.us-cert.gov/awareness/awareness-home

NIH Information Security Awareness Course

http://irtsectraining.nih.gov/

National Cyber Security Awareness Month

https://www.dhs.gov/national-cyber-security-awareness-month

Cyber Security Tips: US-CERT

http://www.us-cert.gov/ncas/tips

Cyber Security Alerts: US-CERT

http://www.us-cert.gov/ncas/alerts

Information Security Awareness Training for Texas

http://www.txdps.state.tx.us/SecurityReview/secAwarenessTraining.pdf

Florida Department of Children and Families

http://www.myflfamilies.com/about-us/dcf-training

Information Security Awareness Training Family Educational Rights and Privacy Act (FERPA)

http://www.uh.edu/legal-affairs/general-counsel/OGC%20Website%20FERPA%20-%20ISAT%20Training.pdf

APPENDIX B: SECURITY AWARENESS TIPS

Stop.Think.Connect

http://www.dhs.gov/stopthinkconnect

StaySafeOnline

http://www.staysafeonline.org/

APPENDIX C: SAMPLE POLICIES

SANS: Information Security Policy Templates

http://www.sans.org/security-resources/policies/

Open-Source Security Awareness Training Resources

Security Awareness Training Framework (SATF) http://www.satframework.org/

APPENDIX D: COMMERCIAL SECURITY AWARENESS TRAINING RESOURCES

SANS: Securing The Human

http://www.securingthehuman.org/

The Security Awareness Company

http://www.thesecurityawarenesscompany.com/

Kevin Mitnick Security Awareness Training: KnowBe4

http://www.knowbe4.com/products/kevin-mitnick-security-awareness-training/

The Roer Group: The Security Culture Company

http://theroergroup.com/

APPENDIX E: OTHER WEB RESOURCES AND LINKS

SANS: The Importance of Security Awareness Training

http://www.sans.org/reading-room/whitepapers/awareness/importance-security-awareness-training-33013

Schneier on Security: Security Awareness Training

https://www.schneier.com/blog/archives/2013/03/security_awaren_1.html

Building a Security Awareness Program: CyberGuard

http://www.gideonrasmussen.com/article-01.html

Security Awareness Toolbox: The Information Warfare Site

http://www.gideonrasmussen.com/article-01.html

SANS Reading Room: Security Awareness Section

http://www.sans.org/reading-room/whitepapers/awareness/?cat=awareness

SECURITY AWARENESS POSTERS

http://www.iwar.org.uk/comsec/resources/ia-awareness-posters/index.htm

Cyber Security Awareness Challenge 2.0

http://iase.disa.mil/eta/cyberchallenge/launchPage.htm

APPENDIX F: TECHNICAL TOOLS THAT CAN BE USED TO TEST SECURITY AWARENESS PROGRAMS

Kali Linux

http://www.kali.org/

Social-Engineer Toolkit

https://www.trustedsec.com/downloads/social-engineer-toolkit/

SpearPhisher

https://www.trustedsec.com/september-2013/introducing-spearphisher-simple-phishing-email-generation-tool/

APPENDIX G: THE SECURITY AWARENESS TRAINING FRAMEWORK

About the Security Awareness Training Framework

Purpose/Project Charter

The Security Awareness Training Framework ("SATF") is a cross-disciplinary program that seeks to provide the guiding principles to establish a common practice for creating and using components within the security awareness domain hierarchy. The SATF seeks to redefine the failed approaches to security awareness by producing a reusable, community-driven, technology-agnostic, and vendor-neutral approach to educating the widest base of stakeholders possible, regardless of role, learning style, experience, or personality type. The SATF mission is to focus solely on the *context* of security awareness and provide aligned stakeholders and content providers a reusable and standard schema to produce the appropriate *content*, at the appropriate time, and to the appropriate audience.

Deliverables

The SATF will focus on a series of initial deliverables, to which failure and success will be measured and adjusted as necessary. The following items are considered to be core deliverables of the SATF program:

A series of vendor-agnostic "how-to guides" based on community-driven research and best practices that will assist interested stakeholders in shaping a security awareness campaign for their organization.

A formal taxonomy of security awareness topics, arranged in a multitier tree structure.

A formal taxonomy of stakeholder roles and occupations, arranged in a multitier tree structure.

A formal taxonomy of regulations and legislation to which security awareness activities are affected, arranged in a multitier tree structure.

A formal taxonomy of learning styles and learning models, arranged in a multitier tree structure.

A formal taxonomy of personality types and personality models, arranged in a multitier tree structure.

A Document Type Definition (DTD) that defines the legal building blocks and hierarchy of an XML or similar markup document for describing and consuming security awareness entities and attributes. The SATF DTD will allow content providers the ability to consume the research of the SATF, identify the characteristics of the specific consumer(s) needing security awareness, and produce content that aligns with the SATF through a consistent and personalized experience.

An algorithm or other methodology to produce a unique permutation from the dimensions of the taxonomies by which security awareness activities will be personalized and delivered.

A series of standardized metrics that reach beyond the current state of security awareness metrics to provide a closed-loop system at various levels of a hierarchy to measure consistently the effectiveness of the security awareness activities and campaigns.

An end user browsable, community-driven wiki site that provides the core components and aspects of security awareness activities within the security awareness domain.

Components and Subteams

To effectively manage the large scope of the effort, subteams and committees will need to be established. Participants may join as many subteams as they wish; however, it is generally recommended to commit to no more than two (2) subteams at any given time. Members of subteams are generally expected to be in attendance to the majority of the subteam functions unless where extenuating circumstances prohibit occasional nonparticipation. Each subteam should nominate one or more members to participate in the general steering meetings, where information is shared among all of the teams.

The following subteams are being proposed to achieve the program deliverables and should be considered fluid as needs dictate:

> Taxonomy/classification team
> Documentation/artifact team
> Research/outreach team
> Communications/social media team

Taxonomy/Classification Team

The taxonomy/classification team will be primarily responsible for establishing the classification of security awareness entities into an ordered system that indicates natural relationships. Borrowed primarily from biological concepts, the purpose of a taxonomy will provide the entity to be consistently classified, facilitating the ease of communicating between two or more parties. The following taxonomies have been identified in the program charter deliverables:

> Security awareness topics (e.g., phishing, pharming, and tailgating)
> Stakeholder roles and occupations (e.g., teacher, accountant, and grandmother)
> Legal, regulatory, and legislative objectives (e.g., PCI DSS, HIPAA, and SOX)
> Learning models and styles (Kolb's, VAK/VARK, and Honey and Mumford's)
> Personality models and styles (Big Five, Myers–Briggs, and DISC)

Documentation/Artifact Team

The documentation/artifact team plays a key role in authoring, formatting, and delivering documentation on behalf of the SATF. As part of the program deliverables, the documentation/artifact team will author the how-to guides, white papers, and other artifacts central to the scope of the SATF program.

Research/Outreach Team

The research/outreach team plays a dual role on behalf of the SATF. First, the research team is chartered with searching and collecting artifacts related to security awareness from around the Internet and through scholarly literature. Secondly, the outreach team is chartered with using the information gathered through research and presenting documentation as part of the overall SATF message. The end goal is to rally support for the SATF through factual dissemination of information through various in-person delivery channels.

Communications/Social Media Team

The communications/social media team is largely responsible for evangelizing the SATF through social media outlets including Facebook, Twitter, and reddit. By actively engaging in dialog in alignment with the SATF goals, the mission of the SATF is reinforced through virtual channels and online presence.

The History of The Security Awareness Training Framework

The Security Awareness Training Framework officially began during the inaugural DerbyCon conference in 2011. Boris Sverdlik (@jadedsecurity) was presenting "Your Perimeter Sucks" to a packed auditorium of security practitioners.

As is the case in many security presentations, the importance of security awareness and end user training was discussed. However, rather than the typical nod and agreement to the statements, a light bulb went off, causing KC Yerrid (@K0nsp1racy) to ask Boris and the audience on how to fix security awareness training. A brief discussion ensued, and Boris challenged KC to fill the gap. KC accepted, and the Security Awareness Training Framework was born.

Over the course of the next couple of months, a handful of practitioners gathered to take this impulsive project and really define the parameters of the effort. On 3 November 2011, Bill Brenner (@BillBrenner70), managing editor of CSO magazine, published a news article about our project, its mission, and goals. The concept was widely accepted and well received, giving credence to the mission of the project.

Throughout 2012, many members have participated and contributed to the project. Despite the temptation to evangelize the project at security conferences, the core group decided to hold off until DerbyCon 2012 as our first official presentation for our work to date. At DerbyCon, we have our sights set very high on what we have been up to for the past 12 calendar months, setting the vision and truly launching this ambitious program into an organic growth opportunity for its members and beneficiaries. We look forward to driving this program forward and hope that people of all walks and experience levels will latch on and help us bring the initiative to fruition.

The Mission of the Security Awareness Training Framework

The mission of the Security Awareness Training Framework (SATF) revolves around the following themes: Primarily, the SATF seeks to create a free and open-source framework that can be used and advanced by practitioners and stakeholders responsible for the information security of sensitive data. We believe this will occur if we can successfully complete three primary goals:

We want to define the components necessary to deliver an effective security awareness program, including scenarios for specialized functions such as developer training and home user education.

We want to study and leverage the delivery mechanisms and various learning styles of individuals to maximize effectiveness of information security awareness.

We want to develop feedback mechanisms and establish candidate metrics to measure the effectiveness of security awareness programs at various levels of granularity.

In order to gain an understanding of these three goals, let's take a look and dissect each of them individually:

Define the Components

If one looks across the spectrum, there are companies in business to deliver information security to organizations and people. However, the content is typically delivered (on a best-case scenario) via the 80/20 rule. What we mean is that about 80% of the content will be on target to a certain extent, and about 20% will be extraneous or not applicable to the audience member. The content is stale and/or presented annually to satisfy an external party. While we are not trying to criticize these companies, we feel that if we clearly delineate the need for watching profit margin, and focus on determining how to maximize the types of content that should be delivered, the end result is a win–win solution for both the trainer and the trainee. This project does not include any provisions that would result in a conflict of interest by offering and/or endorsing a product solution that would benefit the project at large.

It is a big initiative, and those that have participated realize the magnitude and the scope of our efforts. To effectively deliver on this project's mission, the project participants need to define what combination of topics is appropriate for people in all geographic areas, within all types of people, with all roles and responsibilities for information security. Examples of questions that we seek to answer are as follows:

What does a home computer user need to know about securing their wireless networks?
Does an accountant in the US automobile industry need to know about PCI DSS?
What should an elementary school teacher be teaching his or her 3rd grade classroom?

Understand how people learn information security awareness

By borrowing a page from education and academia, the Security Awareness Training Framework seeks to study how people learn security awareness the best. We suspect that people have a preferred learning style; some are visual learners, while some are tactile or kinesthetic learners. There are a number of academic models that attempt to categorize learning styles. The SATF seeks to add a dimension that is often overlooked, particularly in the corporate sector: customized delivery to maximize effectiveness of the program. Many of us have participated in training sessions, whether computer-based training or instructor-led, that made us feel bored, distracted, or not very interested in learning.

The SATF will add that specific dimension to the content that is defined by providing recommendations, materials, and empirical data to support why a one-size-fits-all training solution is inefficient. The bottom line is that if the stakeholder is engaged with applicable content that is tailored to his or her individual learning style, the chances of knowledge retention are increased significantly, while the residual risk is lowered dramatically.

Examples of some of the questions the project seeks to answer include the following:

For visual learners, what font family and size text is best for an audience of 25 people?

For kinesthetic learners, does an e-mail sent by a manager increase or decrease the chance of a successful phishing attempt?

How does voice inflection affect training efficacy?

Develop feedback mechanisms and standardized reporting metrics

In the spirit of ensuring the Security Awareness Training Framework is a living and perpetual endeavor, the project team is seeking to define the appropriate feedback mechanisms that ensure confidentiality and integrity of reporting the effectiveness of the security awareness program as it is deployed via the various use cases. Historically, very few metrics have existed to accurately identify the effectiveness of a security awareness program. Our goal is to provide the clarity and transparency necessary to allow a person, a group of people, an organization, or a collective industry to measure how the framework is working over time. Based on the information collected in metrics, the stakeholders can make actionable decisions based on the effectiveness of the security awareness program. Examples of questions that we seek to answer are as follows:

Is my organization more aware of appropriate security measures than they were last month?

What percentage of targets clicked on a specific phishing message during a simulation?

How satisfied are the people with the security awareness program compared to a baseline?

In so many ways, it sometimes feels as though we are trying to boil the ocean with lofty and impossible goals. However, as the famous saying goes, the best way to eat an elephant is to take 1 bite at a time. The more people that we have contributing to our program wiki, the more we can collectively accomplish. Want to get involved? Contact us!

Source: http://www.satframework.org/

APPENDIX H: BUILDING A SECURITY AWARENESS TRAINING PROGRAM OUTLINE

- What is security awareness training?
- Why does your organization need a security awareness program?
- Getting management buy-in
  - Policy development
  - Policy enforcement
  - Cost savings
  - Production increases
- In order to properly train users, they must first understand the threats.
  - Motivations of cyber criminals
  - Money
  - Industrial espionage/trade secrets
  - Hacktivism
  - Cyber war
  - Bragging rights
- Costs of cleaning up after a breach (Ponemon Institute)
  - Organized crime
  - Nation-states
  - Hacking gangs
  - Hacktivist
  - Cyber war
- Most attacks are targeted.
  - Targeted by application
  - Targeted by OS targeted via phishing, 0day, and ports
  - Targeted as an industry
- Everyone is responsible for security.
  - Education is key to security.

- Countermeasures
  - Passwords
  - Locking computers
  - Attachments
  - Phishing
  - Social engineering
- Security awareness is the only known defense to social engineering.
  - Not all security breaches are the result of technical attack.
  - In information security, people are the weakest link.
- No tech hacking
  - Dumpster diving
  - Tailgating
  - Shoulder surfing
  - Google hacking
  - P2P hacking
- Insecure third-party software
  - P2P file sharing
  - Instant messaging
  - Adware
  - Spyware
  - Web attacks
- Recent examples of web attacks
- Data leakage
- Metadata awareness
  - Track changes/redlining
- Training cycle
  - New hire
  - Quarterly
  - Yearly
  - Continual
- Training types
  - In-person
  - Online
  - Classroom
  - Formal
  - Informal
- Building engaging training
  - Social engineering users
  - Social engineering management
  - One-on-one interaction
  - Penalty cards
  - Reward-based interaction

- ○ Continual message
- ○ Awareness posters
- ○ Desktop backgrounds
- ○ E-mail campaigns
- ○ Using Security Awareness Month
- ○ Organization-wide intensive training
- ○ Special events
- ○ Must be engaging
- • Metrics
  - ○ Measuring training effectiveness
    - – Help desk tickets
    - – Incident response
    - – Are using asking better questions?
- • Why most security awareness programs suck?
  - ○ Don't engage the user.
  - ○ Canned programs are the worst.
  - ○ Overly complicated.
  - ○ Expensive.
  - ○ One size does not fit all.
  - ○ Messages must be targeted.

APPENDIX I: STATE SECURITY BREACH NOTIFICATION LAWS

State	Citation
Alaska	Alaska Stat. § 45.48.010 *et seq.*
Arizona	Ariz. Rev. Stat. § 44-7501
Arkansas	Ark. Code § 4-110-101 *et seq.*
California	Cal. Civ. Code §§ 1798.29, 1798.80 *et seq.*
Colorado	Colo. Rev. Stat. § 6-1-716
Connecticut	Conn. Gen Stat. § 36a-701b
Delaware	Del. Code tit. 6, § 12B-101 *et seq.*
Florida	Fla. Stat. § 817.5681
Georgia	Ga. Code §§ 10-1-910, -911, -912; § 46-5-214
Hawaii	Haw. Rev. Stat. § 487N-1 *et seq.*
Idaho	Idaho Stat. §§ 28-51-104 to -107
Illinois	815 ILCS §§ 530/1 to 530/25
Indiana	Ind. Code §§ 4-1-11 *et seq.*, 24-4.9 *et seq.*
Iowa	Iowa Code §§ 715C.1, 715C.2
Kansas	Kan. Stat. § 50-7a01 *et seq.*
Kentucky	2014 H.B. 5, H.B. 232
Louisiana	La. Rev. Stat. § 51:3071 *et seq.*

Maine	Me. Rev. Stat. tit. 10 §1347 *et seq.*
Maryland	Md. Code Com. Law §§ 14-3501 *et seq.*, Md. State Govt. Code §§ 10-1301 to -1308
Massachusetts	Mass. Gen. Laws §93H-1 *et seq.*
Michigan	Mich. Comp. Laws §§445.63, 445.72
Minnesota	Minn. Stat. §§325E.61, 325E.64
Mississippi	Miss. Code § 75-24-29
Missouri	Mo. Rev. Stat. §407.1500
Montana	Mont. Code §2-6-504, 30-14-1701 *et seq.*
Nebraska	Neb. Rev. Stat. §§87-801, -802, -803, -804, -805, -806, -807
Nevada	Nev. Rev. Stat. §§ 603A.010 *et seq.*, 242.183
New Hampshire	N.H. Rev. Stat. §§359-C:19, -C:20, -C:21
New Jersey	N.J. Stat. §56:8-163
New York	N.Y. Gen. Bus. Law § 899-aa, N.Y. State Tech. Law 208
North Carolina	N.C. Gen. Stat §§75-61, 75-65
North Dakota	N.D. Cent. Code §51-30-01 *et seq.*
Ohio	Ohio Rev. Code §§1347.12, 1349.19, 1349.191, 1349.192
Oklahoma	Okla. Stat. §§74-3113.1, 24-161 to -166
Oregon	Oregon Rev. Stat. §646A.600 *et seq.*
Pennsylvania	73 Pa. Stat. § 2301 *et seq.*
Rhode Island	R.I. Gen. Laws §11-49.2-1 *et seq.*
South Carolina	S.C. Code §39-1-90, 2013 H.B. 3248
Tennessee	Tenn. Code § 47-18-2107
Texas	Tex. Bus. & Com. Code §§521.002, 521.053, Tex. Ed. Code § 37.007(b)(5)
Utah	Utah Code §§ 13-44-101 *et seq.*
Vermont	Vt. Stat. tit. 9 §2430, 2435
Virginia	Va. Code §18.2-186.6, §32.1-127.1:05
Washington	Wash. Rev. Code §19.255.010, 42.56.590
West Virginia	W.V. Code §§46A-2A-101 *et seq.*
Wisconsin	Wis. Stat. §134.98
Wyoming	Wyo. Stat. §40-12-501 *et seq.*
District of Columbia	D.C. Code § 28-3851 *et seq.*
Guam	9 GCA § 48-10 *et seq.*
Puerto Rico	10 Laws of Puerto Rico § 4051 *et seq.*
Virgin Islands	V.I. Code tit. 14, § 2208

States with no security breach law: Alabama, New Mexico, and South Dakota

Source: http://www.ncsl.org/research/telecommunications-and-information-technology/security-breach-notification-laws.aspx

APPENDIX J: WEST VIRGINIA STATE BREACH NOTIFICATION LAWS, W.V. CODE §§46A-2A-101 ET SEQ

CHAPTER 46A. WEST VIRGINIA CONSUMER CREDIT AND PROTECTION ACT

Article 2a. Breach of Security of Consumer Information

§46A-2A-101. Definitions

As used in this article:

(1) "Breach of the security of a system" means the unauthorized access and acquisition of unencrypted and unredacted computerized data that compromises the security or confidentiality of personal information maintained by an individual or entity as part of a database of personal information regarding multiple individuals and that causes the individual or entity to reasonably believe that the breach of security has caused or will cause identity theft or other fraud to any resident of this state. Good faith acquisition of personal information by an employee or agent of an individual or entity for the purposes of the individual or the entity is not a breach of the security of the system, provided that the personal information is not used for a purpose other than a lawful purpose of the individual or entity or subject to further unauthorized disclosure.

(2) "Entity" includes corporations, business trusts, estates, partnerships, limited partnerships, limited liability partnerships, limited liability companies, associations, organizations, joint ventures, governments, governmental subdivisions, agencies, or instrumentalities, or any other legal entity, whether for profit or not for profit.

(3) "Encrypted" means transformation of data through the use of an algorithmic process to into a form in which there is a low probability of assigning meaning without use of a confidential process or key or securing the information by another method that renders the data elements unreadable or unusable.

(4) "Financial institution" has the meaning given that term in Section 6809(3), US Code Title 15, as amended.

(5) "Individual" means a natural person.

(6) "Personal information" means the first name or first initial and last name linked to any one or more of the following data elements that relate to a resident of this state, when the data elements are neither encrypted nor redacted:

(A) Social Security number

(B) Driver's license number or state identification card number issued in lieu of a driver's license

(C) Financial account number, or credit card, or debit card number in combination with any required security code, access code, or password that would permit access to a resident's financial accounts.

The term does not include information that is lawfully obtained from publicly available information or from federal, state, or local government records lawfully made available to the general public.

(7) "Notice" means the following:

(A) Written notice to the postal address in the records of the individual or entity

(B) Telephonic notice

(C) Electronic notice, if the notice provided is consistent with the provisions regarding electronic records and signatures, set forth in Section 7001, US Code Title 15, Electronic Signatures in Global and National Commerce Act

(D) Substitute notice, if the individual or the entity required to provide notice demonstrates that the cost of providing notice will exceed fifty thousand dollars or that the affected class of residents to be notified exceeds one hundred thousand persons or that the individual or the entity does not have sufficient contact information or to provide notice as described in paragraph (A), (B), or (C). Substitute notice consists of any two of the following:

    (i) E-mail notice if the individual or the entity has e-mail addresses for the members of the affected class of residents

    (ii) Conspicuous posting of the notice on the website of the individual or the entity if the individual or the entity maintains a website

    (iii) Notice to major statewide media

(8) "Redact" means alteration or truncation of data such that no more than the last four digits of a Social Security number, driver's license number, state identification card number, or account number are accessible as part of the personal information.

§46A-2A-102. Notice of breach of security of computerized personal information

(a) An individual or entity that owns or licenses computerized data that include personal information shall give notice of any breach of the security of the system following discovery or notification of the breach of the security of the system to any resident of this state whose unencrypted and unredacted personal information was or is reasonably believed to have been accessed and acquired by an unauthorized person and that causes, or the individual or entity reasonably believes has caused or will cause, identity theft or other fraud to any resident of this state. Except as provided in subsection (e) of this section or in order to take any measures necessary to determine the scope of the breach and to restore the reasonable integrity of the system, the notice shall be made without unreasonable delay.

(b) An individual or entity must give notice of the breach of the security of the system if encrypted information is accessed and acquired in an unencrypted form or if the security breach involves a person with access to the encryption key and the individual or entity reasonably believes that such breach has caused or will cause identity theft or other fraud to any resident of this state.

(c) An individual or entity that maintains computerized data that include personal information that the individual or entity does not own or license shall give notice to the owner or licensee of the information of any breach of the security of the system as soon as practicable following discovery, if the personal information was or the entity reasonably believes was accessed and acquired by an unauthorized person.

(d) The notice shall include the following:

    (1) To the extent possible, a description of the categories of information that were reasonably believed to have been accessed or acquired by an unauthorized person, including Social Security numbers, driver's licenses, or state identification numbers and financial data

    (2) A telephone number or website address that the individual may use to contact the entity or the agent of the entity and from whom the individual may learn the following:

        (A) What types of information the entity maintained about that individual or about individuals in general

        (B) Whether or not the entity maintained information about that individual

    (3) The toll-free contact telephone numbers and addresses for the major credit reporting agencies and information on how to place a fraud alert or security freeze

(e) Notice required by this section may be delayed if a law enforcement agency determines and advises the individual or entity that the notice will impede a criminal or civil

Continued

CHAPTER 46A. WEST VIRGINIA CONSUMER CREDIT AND PROTECTION ACT—CONT'D

investigation or homeland or national security. Notice required by this section must be made without unreasonable delay after the law enforcement agency determines that notification will no longer impede the investigation or jeopardize national or homeland security.

(f) If an entity is required to notify more than one thousand persons of a breach of security pursuant to this article, the entity shall also notify, without unreasonable delay, all consumer reporting agencies that compile and maintain files on a nationwide basis, as defined by 15 U.S.C. §1681a (p), of the timing, distribution, and content of the notices. Nothing in this subsection shall be construed to require the entity to provide to the consumer reporting agency the names or other personal identifying information of breach notice recipients. This subsection shall not apply to an entity who is subject to Title V of the Gramm Leach Bliley Act, 15 U.S.C. 6801, *et seq.*

(g) The notice required by this section shall not be considered a debt communication as defined by the Fair Debt Collection Practice Act in 15 U.S.C. §1692a.

§46A-2A-103. Procedures deemed in compliance with security breach notice requirements

(a) An entity that maintains its own notification procedures as part of an information privacy or security policy for the treatment of personal information and that is consistent with the timing requirements of this article shall be deemed to be in compliance with the notification requirements of this article if it notifies residents of this state in accordance with its procedures in the event of a breach of security of the system.

(b) A financial institution that responds in accordance with the notification guidelines prescribed by the Federal Interagency Guidance on Response Programs for Unauthorized Access to Customer Information and Customer Notice is deemed to be in compliance with this article.

(c) An entity that complies with the notification requirements or procedures pursuant to the rules, regulation, procedures, or guidelines established by the entity's primary or functional regulator shall be in compliance with this article.

§46A-2A-104. Violations

(a) Except as provided by subsection (c) of this section, failure to comply with the notice provisions of this article constitutes an unfair or deceptive act of practice in violation of section one hundred four, article six, chapter forty-six-a of this code, which may be enforced by the attorney general pursuant to the enforcement provisions of this chapter.

(b) Except as provided by subsection (c) of this section, the attorney general shall have exclusive authority to bring action. No civil penalty may be assessed in an action unless the court finds that the defendant has engaged in a course of repeated and willful violations of this article. No civil penalty shall exceed one hundred fifty thousand dollars per breach of security of the system or series of breaches of a similar nature that are discovered in a single investigation.

(c) A violation of this article by a licensed financial institution shall be enforceable exclusively by the financial institution's primary functional regulator.

§46A-2A-105. Applicability

This article shall apply to the discovery or notification of a breach of the security of the system that occurs on or after the effective date of this article.

Source: http://www.legis.state.wv.us/WVCODE/Code.cfm?chap=46a&art=2A#2A.

APPENDIX K: HIPAA BREACH NOTIFICATION RULE

The HIPAA Breach Notification Rule, 45 CFR §§ 164.400-414, requires HIPAA-covered entities and their business associates to provide notification following a breach of unsecured protected health information. Similar breach notification provisions implemented and enforced by the Federal Trade Commission (FTC) apply to vendors of personal health records and their third-party service providers, pursuant to Section 13407 of the HITECH Act.

Definition of Breach

A breach is, generally, an impermissible use or disclosure under the Privacy Rule that compromises the security or privacy of protected health information. An impermissible use or disclosure of protected health information is presumed to be a breach unless the covered entity or business associate, as applicable, demonstrates that there is a low probability that protected health information has been compromised based on a risk assessment of at least the following factors:

1. The nature and extent of protected health information involved, including the types of identifiers and the likelihood of reidentification
2. The unauthorized person who used protected health information or to whom the disclosure was made
3. Whether protected health information was actually acquired or viewed
4. The extent to which the risk to protected health information has been mitigated

Covered entities and business associates, where applicable, have discretion to provide the required breach notifications following an impermissible use or disclosure without performing a risk assessment to determine the probability that protected health information has been compromised.

There are three exceptions to the definition of "breach." The first exception applies to the unintentional acquisition, access, or use of protected health information by a workforce member or person acting under the authority of a covered entity or business associate, if such acquisition, access, or use was made in good faith and within the scope of authority. The second exception applies to the inadvertent disclosure of protected health information by a person authorized to access protected health information at a covered entity or business associate to another person authorized to access protected health information at the covered entity or business associate or organized healthcare arrangement in which the covered entity participates. In both cases, the information cannot be further used or disclosed in a manner not permitted by the Privacy Rule. The final exception applies if the covered entity or business associate has a good faith belief that the unauthorized person to whom the impermissible disclosure was made would not have been able to retain the information.

Unsecured Protected Health Information and Guidance

Covered entities and business associates must only provide the required notifications if the breach involved unsecured protected health information. Unsecured protected health information is protected health information that has not been rendered unusable, unreadable, or indecipherable to unauthorized persons through the use of a technology or methodology specified by the secretary in guidance.

This guidance was first issued in April 2009 with a request for public comment. The guidance was reissued after consideration of public comment received and specifies encryption and destruction as the technologies and methodologies for rendering protected health information unusable, unreadable, or indecipherable to unauthorized individuals. Additionally, the guidance also applies to unsecured personal health record identifiable health information under the FTC regulations. Covered entities and business associates, as well as entities regulated by the FTC regulations, that secure information as specified by the guidance are relieved from providing notifications following the breach of such information.

Breach Notification Requirements

Following a breach of unsecured protected health information, covered entities must provide notification of the breach to the affected individuals, the secretary, and, in certain circumstances, the media. In addition, business associates must notify covered entities if a breach occurs at or by the business associate.

Individual Notice

Covered entities must notify the affected individuals following the discovery of a breach of unsecured protected health information. Covered entities must provide this individual notice in written form by first-class mail or, alternatively, by e-mail if the affected individual has agreed to receive such notices electronically. If the covered entity has insufficient or out-of-date contact information for 10 or more individuals, the covered entity must provide substitute individual notice by either posting the notice on the home page of its website for at least 90 days or providing the notice in major print or broadcast media where the affected individuals likely reside. The covered entity must include a toll-free phone number that remains active for at least 90 days where individuals can learn if their information was involved in the breach. If the covered entity has insufficient or out-of-date contact information for fewer than

10 individuals, the covered entity may provide substitute notice by an alternative form of written notice, by telephone, or by other means.

These individual notifications must be provided without unreasonable delay and in no case later than 60 days following the discovery of a breach and must include, to the extent possible, a brief description of the breach; a description of the types of information that were involved in the breach; the steps affected individuals should take to protect themselves from potential harm; a brief description of what the covered entity is doing to investigate the breach, mitigate the harm, and prevent further breaches; and contact information for the covered entity (or business associate, as applicable).

With respect to a breach at or by a business associate, while the covered entity is ultimately responsible for ensuring individuals are notified, the covered entity may delegate the responsibility of providing individual notices to the business associate. Covered entities and business associates should consider which entity is in the best position to provide notice to the individual, which may depend on various circumstances, such as the functions the business associate performs on behalf of the covered entity and which entity has the relationship with the individual.

Media Notice

Covered entities that experience a breach affecting more than 500 residents of a state or jurisdiction are, in addition to notifying the affected individuals, required to provide notice to prominent media outlets serving the state or jurisdiction. Covered entities will likely provide this notification in the form of a press release to appropriate media outlets serving the affected area. Like individual notice, this media notification must be provided without unreasonable delay and in no case later than 60 days following the discovery of a breach and must include the same information required for the individual notice.

Notice to the Secretary

In addition to notifying affected individuals and the media (where appropriate), covered entities must notify the secretary of breaches of unsecured protected health information. Covered entities will notify the secretary by visiting the HHS website (http://www.hhs.gov/ocr/privacy/hipaa/administrative/breachnotificationrule/brinstruction.html) and filling out and electronically submitting a breach report form. If a breach affects 500 or more individuals, covered entities must notify the secretary without unreasonable delay and in no case later than 60 days following a breach. If, however, a breach affects fewer than 500 individuals, the covered entity may notify the secretary of such breaches on an annual basis. Reports of breaches affecting fewer than

500 individuals are due to the secretary no later than 60 days after the end of the calendar year in which the breaches are discovered.

NOTIFICATION BY A BUSINESS ASSOCIATE

If a breach of unsecured protected health information occurs at or by a business associate, the business associate must notify the covered entity following the discovery of the breach. A business associate must provide notice to the covered entity without unreasonable delay and no later than 60 days from the discovery of the breach. To the extent possible, the business associate should provide the covered entity with the identification of each individual affected by the breach as well as any other available information required to be provided by the covered entity in its notification to affected individuals.

Administrative Requirements and Burden of Proof

Covered entities and business associates, as applicable, have the burden of demonstrating that all required notifications have been provided or that a use or disclosure of unsecured protected health information did not constitute a breach. Thus, with respect to an impermissible use or disclosure, a covered entity (or business associate) should maintain documentation that all required notifications were made or, alternatively, documentation to demonstrate that notification was not required: (1) its risk assessment demonstrating a low probability that protected health information has been compromised by the impermissible use or disclosure or (2) the application of any other exceptions to the definition of "breach."

Covered entities are also required to comply with certain administrative requirements with respect to breach notification. For example, covered entities must have in place written policies and procedures regarding breach notification, must train employees on these policies and procedures, and must develop and apply appropriate sanctions against workforce members who do not comply with these policies and procedures.

Source: http://www.hhs.gov/ocr/privacy/hipaa/administrative/breachnotificationrule/

Instructions for Submitting Notice of a Breach to the Secretary

The breach notification rule requires covered entities to provide the secretary with notice of breaches of unsecured protected health information (45 CFR 164.408). All notifications must be submitted to the secretary using the OCR submission portal below. The number of individuals affected by the breach determines when the notification must be submitted to the secretary. Please review the instructions below for submitting breach notifications.

Breaches Affecting 500 or More Individuals

If a breach affects 500 or more individuals, a covered entity must provide the secretary with notice of the breach without unreasonable delay and in no case later than 60 days from discovery of the breach. This notice must be submitted electronically by following the link below and completing all information required on the breach notification form.

If a covered entity that has submitted a breach notification form to the secretary discovers additional information to report, the covered entity may submit an additional form, checking the appropriate box to signal that it is an updated submission. If, at the time of submission of the form, it is unclear how many individuals are affected by a breach, please provide an estimate of the number of individuals affected. As this information becomes available, an additional breach report may be submitted as an addendum to the initial report.

For questions regarding the completion and submission of this form, please e-mail OCRPrivacy@hhs.gov.

Breaches Affecting Fewer than 500 Individuals

For breaches that affect fewer than 500 individuals, a covered entity must provide the secretary with notice of breaches within 60 days of the end of the calendar year in which the breaches were discovered. This notice must be submitted electronically by following the link below and completing all information required on the breach notification form. A separate form must be completed for every breach that was discovered during the calendar year.

If a covered entity that has submitted a breach notification form to the secretary discovers additional information to report, the covered entity may submit an additional form, checking the appropriate box to signal that it is an updated submission. If, at the time of submission of the form, it is unclear how many individuals are affected by a breach, please provide an estimate of the number of individuals affected. As this information becomes available, an additional breach report may be submitted as an addendum to the initial report.

For questions regarding the completion and submission of this form, please e-mail OCRPrivacy@hhs.gov.

Source: http://www.hhs.gov/ocr/privacy/hipaa/administrative/breachnotificationrule/brinstruction.html

FEDERAL TRADE COMMISSION (FTC) HEALTH BREACH NOTIFICATION RULE

Does your business or organization have a website that allows people to maintain their medical information online? Do you provide applications for personal health records—say, a device that allows people to upload readings from a blood pressure cuff or pedometer into their personal health record?

The American Recovery and Reinvestment Act of 2009 includes provisions to strengthen privacy and security protections for this new sector of web-based businesses. The law directed the Federal Trade Commission to issue a rule requiring companies to contact customers in the event of a security breach. After receiving comments from the public, the FTC issued the Health Breach Notification Rule.

Under the FTC rule, companies that have had a security breach must

1. notify everyone whose information was breached;
2. in many cases, notify the media; and
3. notify the FTC.

The FTC has designed a standard form for companies to use to notify the FTC of a breach and periodically posts a list of breaches for which it received notice under the rule. A brochure for businesses, complying with the FTC Health Breach Notification Rule, explains who's covered by the rule and offers guidance on what to do in case of a breach. FTC enforcement began on 22 February 2010.

The FTC Health Breach Notification Rule applies only to health information that is not secured through technologies specified by the Department of Health and Human Services. Also, the FTC rule does not apply to businesses or organizations covered by the Health Insurance Portability and Accountability Act (HIPAA). In case of a security breach, entities covered by HIPAA must comply with the HHS Breach Notification Rule.

Source: http://business.ftc.gov/privacy-and-security/health-privacy/health-breach-notification-rule

APPENDIX L: COMPLYING WITH THE FTC HEALTH BREACH NOTIFICATION RULE

More and more, personal medical information is online. For most hospitals, doctors' offices, and insurance companies, the Health Insurance Portability and Accountability Act (HIPAA) governs the privacy and security of health records stored online. But many web-based businesses that collect people's health information aren't covered by HIPAA. These include online services people use to keep track of their health information and online applications that interact with those services.

The Federal Trade Commission (FTC), the nation's consumer protection agency, has issued the Health Breach Notification Rule to require certain businesses not covered by HIPAA to notify their customers and others if there's a breach of unsecured, individually identifiable electronic health information. FTC enforcement began on 22 February 2010.

Is your business covered by the Health Breach Notification Rule? Do you know your legal obligations if you experience a security breach?

WHO'S COVERED BY THE HEALTH BREACH NOTIFICATION RULE

The rule applies if you are

a vendor of personal health records (PHRs),
a PHR-related entity, or
a third-party service provider for a vendor of PHRs or a PHR-related entity.

Vendor of personal health records. For the purposes of the rule, your business is a vendor of personal health records if it "offers or maintains a personal health record." A personal health record is defined as an electronic record of "identifiable health information on an individual that can be drawn from multiple sources and that is managed, shared, and controlled by or primarily for the individual." For example, if you have an online service that allows consumers to store and organize medical information from many sources in one online location, you're a vendor of personal health records.

YOU'RE NOT A VENDOR OF PERSONAL HEALTH RECORDS IF YOU'RE COVERED BY HIPAA

PHR-related entity. Your business is a PHR-related entity if it interacts with a vendor of personal health records either by offering products or services through the vendor's website—even if the site is covered by HIPAA—or by accessing information in a personal health record or sending information to a personal health record. Many businesses that offer web-based apps for health information fall into this category. For example, if you have an app that helps consumers manage their medications or lets them upload readings from a device like a blood pressure cuff or pedometer into a personal health record, your business is a PHR-related entity. However, if consumers can simply input their own information on your site in a way that doesn't interact with personal health records offered by a vendor—for example, if your site just allows consumers to input their weight each week to track their fitness goals—you're not a PHR-related entity. You're not a PHR-related entity if you're already covered by HIPAA.

THIRD-PARTY SERVICE PROVIDER

Your business is a third-party service provider if it offers services involving the use, maintenance, disclosure, or disposal of health information to vendors of personal health records or PHR-related entities. For example, if a vendor of personal health records hires your business to provide billing, debt collection, or data storage services related to health information, you're a third-party service provider and covered by the rule.

WHAT TRIGGERS THE NOTIFICATION REQUIREMENT

The rule requires that you provide notice when there has been an unauthorized acquisition of PHR-identifiable health information that is unsecured and in a personal health record. How those terms are defined is important:

Unauthorized acquisition. If the health information that you maintain or use is acquired by someone else without the affected person's approval, it's an unauthorized acquisition under the rule. For example, a thief steals an employee's laptop containing unsecured personal health records or someone on your staff downloads personal health records without approval. Those are probably unauthorized acquisitions that trigger the rule's notification requirement.

PHR-identifiable health information. The notification requirements apply only when you've experienced a breach of PHR-identifiable health information. This is health information that identifies someone or could reasonably be used to identify someone. For example, someone hacks into a company database that contains zip codes, dates of birth, and medication information. Even though the database didn't contain names, it would be reasonable to believe the information could be used to identify people in the database. But what if a hacker gains access to a database that contains only city and medication data and finds out that ten anonymous individuals in New York City have been prescribed a widely used drug? That probably wouldn't be considered PHR-identifiable health information because it couldn't reasonably be used to identify specific people.

Unsecured information. The rule applies only to unsecured health information, defined by the US Department of Health and Human Services (HHS) to include any information that is not encrypted or destroyed. If your employee loses a laptop containing only encrypted personal health records, for example, you wouldn't be required to provide notification.

Personal health record. A personal health record is an electronic health record that can be "drawn from multiple sources and that is managed, shared, and controlled by or primarily for the individual." If your business experiences a breach involving only paper health records—not electronic records—the FTC rule doesn't require any notification. However, because many states have notification laws that might apply, it's wise to consult your attorney.

WHAT TO DO IF A BREACH OCCURS

If your business is a vendor of personal health records or a PHR-related entity and there's a security breach, the rule spells out your next steps. You must notify

    each affected person who is a citizen or resident of the United States;
    the Federal Trade Commission; and,
    in some cases, the media.

Here are the details of the rule's main requirements about who you must notify and when you must notify them, how you must notify them, and what information to include.

WHO YOU MUST NOTIFY AND WHEN YOU MUST NOTIFY THEM

People: If you experience a breach of unsecured personal health information, you must notify each affected person "without unreasonable delay" and within 60 calendar days after the breach is discovered. The countdown begins the day the breach becomes known to someone in your company—or the day someone should reasonably have known about it. Although the rule requires you to notify people within 60 calendar days, it also requires you to act without unreasonable delay. That means if a company discovers a breach and gathers the necessary information within, say, 30 days, it is unreasonable to wait until the 60th day to notify the people whose information was breached.

The FTC: The rule requires you to notify the FTC, but the timing depends on the number of people affected.

If the breach involves the information of 500 people or more, you must notify the FTC as soon as possible and within 10 business days after discovering the breach. To report the breach to the agency, you must use the form at www.ftc.gov/healthbreach.

If the breach involves the information of fewer than 500 people, you have more time. Indeed, you must send the same standard form to the FTC—along with forms documenting any other breaches during the same calendar year involving fewer than 500 people—within 60 calendar days following the end of the calendar year. So, if your company experiences one breach in April affecting the records of 100 people and a second breach in September affecting the records of 50 people, the 60-day countdown begins January 1st of the next year.

The media: When at least 500 residents of a particular state, the District of Columbia, or a US territory or possession are affected by a breach, notification takes on an extra dimension. Without unreasonable delay—and within 60 calendar days after the breach is discovered—you must notify prominent media outlets serving the relevant locale, including Internet media where appropriate. This media notice is a supplement to your notice to people whose information was breached, not a substitute for individual notices.

If your company is a third-party service provider to a vendor of personal health records or a PHR-related entity, you have notice requirements under the rule, too. As a preliminary matter, the rule requires those clients to tell you up front that they're covered by the rule. If you experience a breach, you must notify an official designated in your contract with your client—or if there is no designee, a senior official of the company—without unreasonable delay and within 60 calendar days of discovering the breach. You must identify for your client each person whose information may be involved in the breach. But it isn't sufficient to simply send the notice and assume the ball is in your client's court. You must get an acknowledgment that they received your notice. They, in turn, must notify the people affected by the breach, the FTC, and, in certain cases, the media.

HOW TO NOTIFY PEOPLE

The best practice in notifying people is to find out from your customers in advance—perhaps when they sign up for your service—if they'd prefer to hear about a security breach by e-mail or by first-class mail. If you collect only e-mail addresses from your customers, you can send them a message—or let new customers know when they sign up—that you intend to contact them by e-mail about any security breaches. However, remember that if you plan to use e-mail as your default method, you must give your customers the opportunity to choose first-class mail notification instead and that option must be clear and conspicuous. If e-mail is a customer's preference, explain how to set up any spam filters so they will get your messages.

What if you've made reasonable efforts to reach people affected by the breach, but you haven't been able to contact each of them? If you fail to contact 10 or more people because of insufficient or out-of-date contact information, you must provide substitute notice through

> a clear and conspicuous posting for 90 days on your home page or
> a notice in major print or broadcast media where those people likely live.

Both of these forms of substitute notice must include a toll-free phone number that has to be active for at least 90 days so people can call to find out if their information was affected by the breach.

WHAT INFORMATION TO INCLUDE

Regardless of the form of notification, your notice to individuals must be easy to understand and must include the following information:

A brief description of what happened, including the date of the breach (if you know) and the date you discovered the breach and the kind of PHR-identifiable health information involved in the breach—insurance information, Social Security numbers, financial account data, dates of birth, medication information, etc.

If the breach puts people at risk for identity theft or other possible harm, suggest steps they can take to protect themselves. Your advice must be relevant to the kind of information that was compromised. In some cases, for example, you may want to refer people to the FTC identity theft website, www.ftc.gov/idtheft.

In addition, if the breach involves health insurance information, you might suggest that people contact their healthcare providers if bills don't arrive on time in case an identity thief has changed the billing address, pay attention to the Explanation of Benefits forms from their insurance company to check for irregularities, and contact their insurance company to notify them of possible medical identity theft or to ask for a new account number.

If the breach includes Social Security numbers, you might suggest that people get a free copy of their credit report from www.annualcreditreport.com, monitor it for signs of identity theft, and place a fraud alert on their credit report. If they spot suspicious activity, they should contact their local police and, if appropriate, get a credit freeze.

If the breach includes financial information—for example, a credit card or bank account number—you might suggest that people monitor their accounts for suspicious activity and contact their financial institution about closing any accounts that may have been compromised.

A brief description of the steps your business is taking to investigate the breach, protect against future breaches, and mitigate the harm from the breach.

How people can contact you for more information. Your notice must include a toll-free telephone number, e-mail address, website, or mailing address.

ANSWERS TO QUESTIONS ABOUT THE HEALTH BREACH NOTIFICATION RULE

Here are answers to some questions businesses have asked about the FTC Health Breach Notification Rule:

Why did the FTC implement the Health Breach Notification Rule?

As part of the American Recovery and Reinvestment Act of 2009—which advances the use of health information technology—Congress directed the FTC and HHS to study potential privacy, security, and breach notification requirements and make recommendations. In the meantime, Congress directed the FTC to implement a temporary rule—the Health Breach Notification Rule—that non-HIPAA businesses must follow if there's a security breach. FTC enforcement began on 22 February 2010.

It looks like someone accessed our database without our consent. We don't know if they downloaded anything. Is that the kind of "unauthorized acquisition" that would trigger the rule's notification requirements?

It should trigger an examination on your part to determine your obligations under the rule. There may be unauthorized access to data, but it's not always clear at first blush whether the data also have been "acquired"—that is, downloaded or copied. In these cases, the rule has a rebuttable presumption: Where there has been unauthorized access, unauthorized acquisition is presumed unless you can show that it hasn't—or couldn't reasonably have—taken place. For example, if one of your employees accesses a customer's personal health record without authorization, the rule presumes that because the data was accessed, it has been "acquired," and you must follow the breach notification provisions of the rule. But you can overcome that presumption by establishing and enforcing a company policy—one that says if an employee inadvertently accesses a health record, he or she must not read or share the information, must log out immediately, and then must report the access to a supervisor right away. If the employee says he or she didn't read or share the information and you conduct a reasonable investigation that corroborates the employee's version of events, you may be able to overcome the presumption.

Consider another situation involving a lost laptop that contains personal health records. You could rebut the presumption of unauthorized acquisition if the laptop is recovered and forensic analysis shows that files were not opened, altered, transferred, or otherwise compromised.

Our business is in the "HIPAA business associate" category. Does the FTC rule apply to us?

If your business acts solely as a "HIPAA business associate"—that is, if you handle only protected health information of HIPAA-covered entities—the FTC rule does not apply. Nor does it apply to HIPAA-covered entities, like a hospital, doctor's office, or health insurance company. If you are an HIPAA-covered entity or act only as an HIPAA business associate, your responsibilities are in the HHS Breach Notification Rule.

The HHS rule requires HIPAA-covered entities to notify people whose unsecured health information is breached. If you are a business associate of an HIPAA-covered entity and you experience a security breach, you must notify the HIPAA-covered entity you're working with. Then, they must notify the people affected by the breach.

WE'RE AN HIPAA BUSINESS ASSOCIATE, BUT WE ALSO OFFER PERSONAL HEALTH RECORD SERVICES TO THE PUBLIC. WHICH RULE APPLIES TO US?

If your company is an HIPAA business associate that also offers personal health record services to the public, you may be subject to both the HHS and the FTC breach notification rules. For example, you have your own website that offers individual customers an online service to collect their health information and you sign an HIPAA business associate agreement with an insurance company to maintain the electronic health records of its customers. In the case of a breach affecting all your users, both the FTC rule and the HHS rule would apply. Under the FTC rule, you must notify the people who use the service on your website. In addition, you must notify the insurance company so that it can notify its customers.

If you have a direct relationship with all the people affected by the breach—your customers and the customers of the insurance company—you should contact the insurance company to notify both your clients and theirs. People are more likely to pay attention to a notice from a company they recognize.

What's the relationship between the FTC Health Breach Notification Rule and the state breach notification laws?

The FTC rule preempts contradictory state breach notification laws, but not those that impose additional—but noncontradictory—breach notification requirements. For example, some state laws require breach notices to include advice on monitoring credit reports or contact information for consumer reporting agencies. While these content requirements are different from the FTC rule requirements, they're not contradictory. In this example, you could comply with both federal and state requirements by including all the information in a single breach notice. The FTC rule doesn't require you to send multiple breach notices to comply with state and federal law.

WHAT'S THE PENALTY FOR VIOLATING THE FTC HEALTH BREACH NOTIFICATION RULE?

The FTC will treat each violation of the rule as an unfair or deceptive act or practice in violation of a Federal Trade Commission regulation. Businesses that violate the rule may be subject to a civil penalty of up to $16,000 per violation.

LAW ENFORCEMENT OFFICIALS HAVE ASKED US TO DELAY NOTIFYING PEOPLE ABOUT THE BREACH. WHAT SHOULD WE DO?

If law enforcement officials determine that notifying people would impede a criminal investigation or damage national security, the rule allows you to delay notifying them, as well as the FTC and, if required, the media.

WHERE CAN I LEARN MORE ABOUT THE FTC HEALTH BREACH NOTIFICATION RULE? VISIT WWW.FTC.GOV/ HEALTHBREACH.

The FTC works to prevent fraudulent, deceptive, and unfair business practices in the marketplace and to provide information to help consumers spot, stop, and avoid them. To file a complaint or get free information on consumer issues, visit ftc.gov or call toll-free, 1-877-FTC-HELP (1-877-382-4357); TTY: 1-866-653-4261. Watch a new video, How to File a Complaint, at ftc.gov/video to learn more. The FTC enters consumer complaints into the Consumer Sentinel Network, a secure online database and investigative tool used by hundreds of civil and criminal law enforcement agencies in the United States and abroad.

YOUR OPPORTUNITY TO COMMENT

The National Small Business Ombudsman and 10 Regional Fairness Boards collect comments from small businesses about federal compliance and enforcement activities. Each year, the ombudsman evaluates the conduct of these activities and rates each agency's responsiveness to small businesses. Small businesses can comment to the ombudsman without fear of reprisal. To comment, call toll-free 1-888-REGFAIR (1-888-734-3247) or go to www.sba.gov/ombudsman.

April 2010

Source: http://business.ftc.gov/documents/bus56-complying-ftcs-health-breach-notification-rule.

APPENDIX L: INFORMATION SECURITY CONFERENCES

The number of information security conferences has grown in recent years. These conferences can be great resources to network with others who are building or have built their own security awareness programs.

Below is a short list of conferences where the authors have spoken or have attended:

DEF CON https://www.defcon.org/
Black Hat https://www.blackhat.com/
ShmoonCon http://www.shmoocon.org/
HOPE http://www.hope.net/
DerbyCon https://www.derbycon.com/
BSidesLV http://www.bsideslv.org/
BSides Charlotte http://bsidesclt.org/
B-Sides Cindy http://bsidescincy.org/
B-Sides DC http://www.bsidesdc.org/
BSides Raleigh http://bsidesraleigh.org/
BSides Asheville http://www.bsidesasheville.com/
BSides Nashville http://www.bsidesnash.org/
BSidesPR http://bsidespr.org/
BSides Austin http://www.BSidesAutin.com
BSides Delaware http://www.securitybsides.com/w/page/28563447/
    BSidesDelaware
BSidesROC http://www.bsidesroc.com/
BSides Huntsville http://www.bsideshuntsville.org/
BSidesCT http://www.securitybsides.com/w/page/73989383/
    BSidesCT2014
BSidesNOLA http://www.securitybsides.com/w/page/62741761/
    BsidesNola
BSidesChicago http://www.securitybsides.com/w/page/70187476/
    BSidesChicago
Hack3rCon http://hack3rcon.org/

THOTCON http://thotcon.org/
Circle City Con http://circlecitycon.com/
AIDE http://www.appyide.org/
CarolinaCon http://carolinacon.org/

APPENDIX M: RECORDED PRESENTATIONS ON HOW TO BUILD AN INFORMATION SECURITY AWARENESS PROGRAM

A Fool's Game: Building an Awareness and Training Program DerbyCon 2012—Brandon Miller and Bill Gardner: http://www.irongeek.com/i.php?page=videos/derbycon2/3-2-5-branden-miller-bill-gardner-building-an-awareness-and-training-program

AIDE 2013: Building an Engaging and Effective Information Security Awareness Program—Bill Gardner http://www.irongeek.com/i.php?page=videos/aide2013/building-an-engaging-and-effective-information-security-awareness-and-training-program-bill-gardner-oncee

Building An Information Security Awareness Program from Scratch—Bill Gardner and Valerie Thomas: DerbyCon 2013 http://www.irongeek.com/i.php?page=videos/derbycon3/5101-building-an-information-security-awareness-program-from-scratch-bill-gardner-valerie-thomas

BSides Cincinnati Bill Gardner—Building A Security Awareness Program https://www.youtube.com/watch?v=zlVHoV1YqGA

APPENDIX N: ARTICLES ON HOW TO BUILD AN INFORMATION SECURITY AWARENESS PROGRAM

How to Offer Security Awareness Training That Works http://www.esecurityplanet.com/network-security/how-to-offer-security-awareness-training-that-works.html?utm_source=dlvr.it&utm_medium=twitter

How Law Firms Can Defend Against Social Engineering http://apps.americanbar.org/litigation/committees/technology/articles/fall2012-1012-how-law-firms-can-defend-against-social-engineering.html

Index

Note: Page numbers followed by *f* indicate figures.

Printed and bound by CPI Group (UK) Ltd, Croydon, CR0 4YY

03/10/2024

01040324-0008